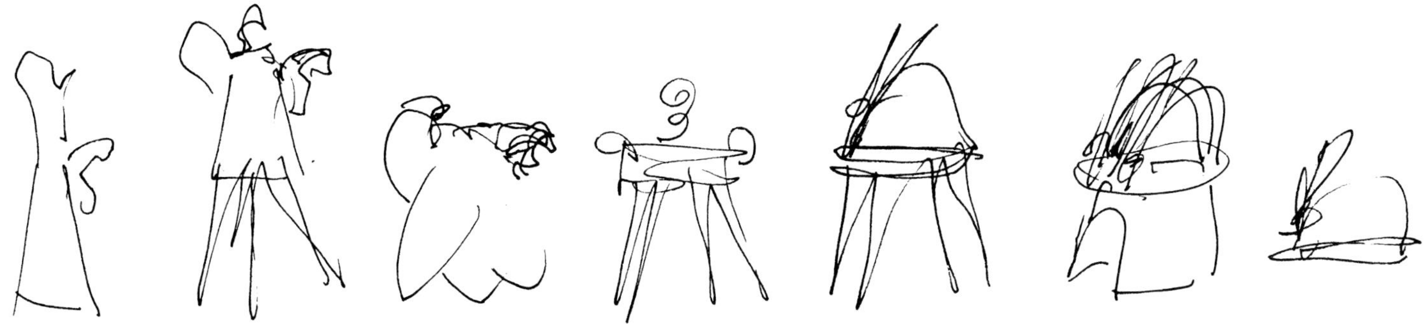

KEN FERGUSON
TALKING WITH THE WHEEL

KEN FERGUSON

GARTH CLARK

JOHN PERREAULT

TED ROWLAND

PETER von ZIEGESAR

KEN FERGUSON

TALKING WITH THE WHEEL

Silver Gate, Inc.
Arlington, TX

KEN FERGUSON TALKING WITH THE WHEEL

2631 Garden Ridge Lane, Arlington, TX

Photography Credits
Gloria Baker-Feinstein: pp. 3, 6, 18, 23, 25 (bottom), 33, 37, 40, 43, 44, 45, 48, 50, 51, 52, 53, 54, 55, 56, 57, 62, 73, 91, 94, 95, 102, 103, 109, 110, and 111.
E.G. Schempf: cover, pp. viii, 10, 11, 12, 14, 16, 19, 20, 21, 22, 25 (top), 29, 30, 31, 34, 38, 39, 42, 46, 58, 60, 63, 64, 67, 68, 69, 70, 71, 74, 75, 76, 77, 78, 79, 82, 83, 85, 86, 87, 88, 89, 92, 96, 97, 104, 105, 106, 107, 108, and 112.
Ken Ferguson: pp. 4 (top right), 4 (bottom), 8, 81, 99 (top left), 99 (bottom), and 100.
Paul Vidal: p. 4 (top left).
Charles K. Unseld: p. 5.
Gertrude Ferguson: dust jacket (interior), p. 7.
Al Abrams: pp. 9, 66.
Anthony Cunha: p. 36.
Jack Ramsdale: p. 42.
U.S. Army photo by PFC James Walker: p 99 (top right).
Charles Ferguson: p 101.

Graphic Design and Production
Cristina Hernández Villalón

Editing
Karen Quarles
Stephanie Gabriels

Printer
Oceanic Graphic Printing
Printed in China

FIRST EDITION

LIBRARY OF CONGRESS CONTROL NUMBER: 2007927097

ISBN 978-0-9791787-0-2

www.silver-gate-inc.com

CONTENTS

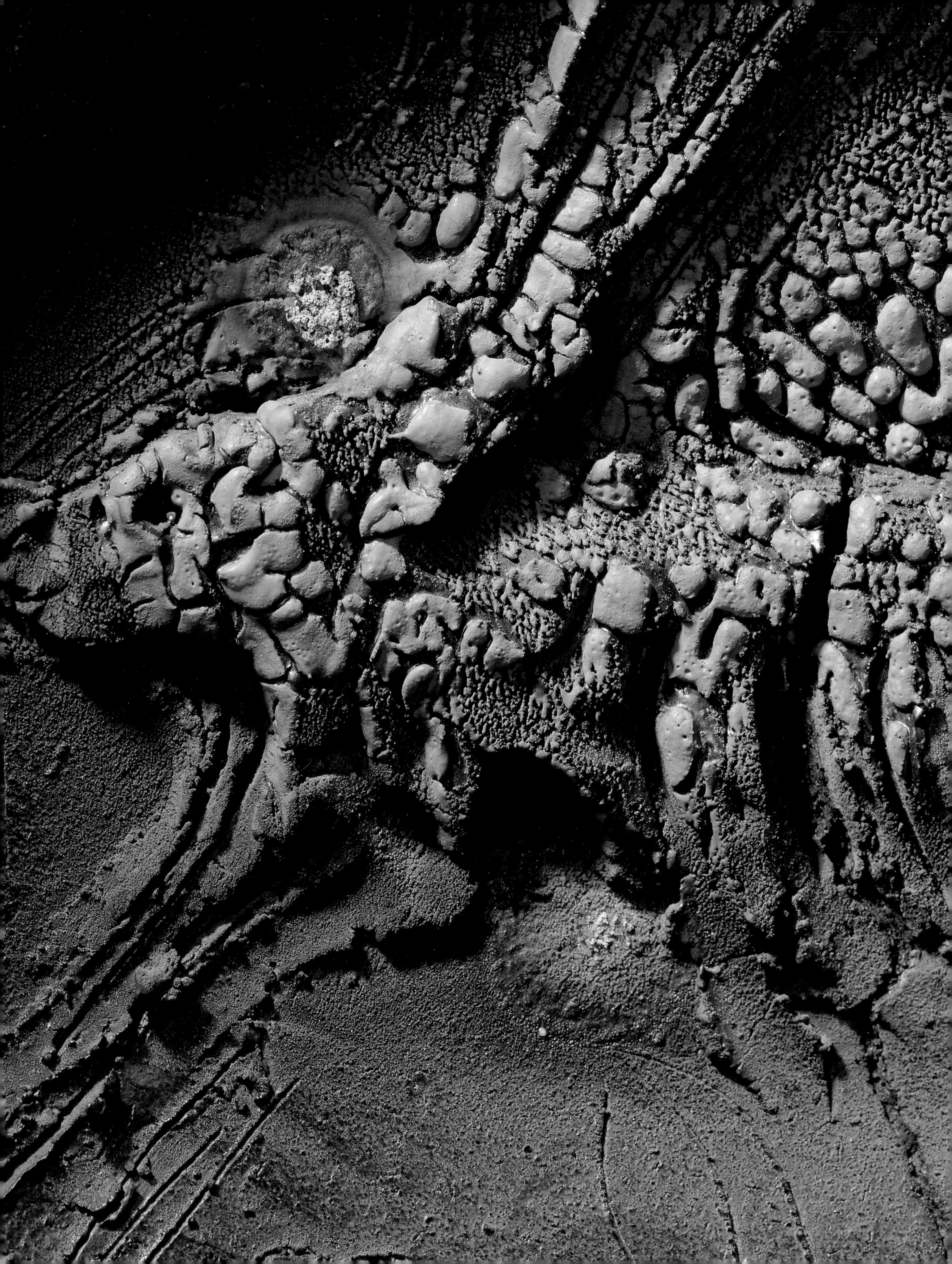

A MATTER OF TIMING

GARTH CLARK

How does the son of a Rust Belt worker become a world-renowned ceramist? Why does he choose ceramics in the first place? How does a man who first fled from art education later become one of the most influential ceramics educators of the twentieth century? The answers to these questions inform us about Ken Ferguson's journey as artist, pedagogue, and agent provocateur, and shed light on the changing place of ceramics in American art. Moreover, when Ferguson took his first steps towards ceramics, it was a precarious career.

Ferguson (as he tends to announce himself on the phone in his booming baritone voice, rarely using his first name) was born on March 6, 1928, in the mill town of Elwood, Indiana. He was the second of two children. The first, his brother, Wallace, was born in 1923. His parents both came from agrarian roots. However, Edith Izora Cockerham, his mother, was not raised on a farm; her family swapped the fields for the factory before she was born. Cecil Ferguson, his father, was of the first generation in his family to abandon the farm life. He was of Scottish and Welsh background—an advantage in seeking factory work. In fact at the time, the tinplate business was run by the Welsh, so he easily found work at a mill that produced tin sheets for Indiana's huge tomato-canning industry.

However, mill-town life possessed little charm. Steady work and livable wages were offset by the long hours and brutish, dangerous nature of the work. Then there was the noise, the loud booming and banging, as well as the vibration of the mills' heavy equipment. The environment was as hard on the workers' wives as the workers—keeping the dirt at bay required a ceaseless effort.

The Fergusons' move to Clairton, Pennsylvania, in 1937, when Ken was nine, brought little change. Despite the soft poetic lilt in the name of the town, it was just another mill town, one of a chain of such communities along the banks of the Monongahela River, radiating from the capital of American steel, Pittsburgh. It later became the gloomy model for the declining Rust Belt town in the movie *The Deer Hunter*. Surprisingly, however, Ken's memories of this company town are not bitter ones. Though life was tough, he recalls a childhood spent playing outdoors in the fields and forests near his home.

There was a deep respect for higher education in the Ferguson family but little interest in art or culture. However, Ken's mother received an oil painting from a friend as a gift, and it was treated as a kind of treasure in the home. Its presence had an impact on Ken as a child; he recalls that it gave him "permission to think about art." His mother was supportive as Ken's interest in the arts grew. His father's only career advice was, "Do anything to avoid the trap of the mill town." Cecil Ferguson viewed the mill town as a kind of prison, and he did not especially care what his sons did with their lives as long as it took them away.

After graduating from high school, Ken worked in the mills for a year but then headed to Chicago and enrolled in the American Academy of Art's summer school. Six weeks later, he returned to Pennsylvania and joined a small, private art school in Pittsburgh better suited to hobbyists than professionals. "I knew nothing at all about art," he recalls, "but I quickly sensed that these schools were not going to give me the grounding and training that I needed. I did not know what to do or where to go next. So I decided to contact my father's cousin, Russell Jennings Ferguson, for guidance. It was perhaps the smartest single thing I did in my life."

Russell and Cecil had grown up together on the farmlands of Indiana. Cecil's mother had died when he was only fifteen, and Russell, slightly older, became a surrogate-older brother. He was viewed by the family with a certain reverence. Like them, Russell had also left the farm, but he had gone into academia rather than industry. When nineteen-year-old Ken sought out his counsel, Russell was established as a distinguished professor of history at the University of Pittsburgh. At their meeting, he confirmed that the schools Ken had been attending were inferior. "At best they will teach you to play a banjo with just one string," he said. "Go to Carnegie Tech and get a fully-rounded education, so you can play all five strings."

The Carnegie Institute of Technology (now Carnegie Mellon University) had already begun its academic year, and the classes were full. Undeterred, Ken attended evening classes for a year while working a full-time day job. He enrolled in the Painting and Design Department the following year. The department head, Wilfred Readio, adjusting Russell's metaphor slightly, announced to the students that his job was not to teach them "how to unlock doors but, rather, how to make keys." What Ken found was an intellectually rigorous department, scrupulously modeled on the principles of the Bauhaus with a soupçon of American pragmatism. He plunged into his studies with confidence, knowing that he was on the right track.

The full tuition fee at Carnegie Tech was $600 per semester, and Ken had to come up with this himself (his friends attending the Pennsylvania State College only had to pay $60). Somehow he managed to support himself through four years of college without assistance from his parents, aside from his board and lodging (he lived at home and commuted to Pittsburgh). During school breaks, he labored morning, noon and night to earn the money to pay for the next semester's tuition.

There were several fellow students from those years who made it to prominence in the art and design world, but by far the most famous was Andy Warhol. The thought of Ferguson—gruff, tough, hulking, and dressed in rough working clothes—next to Warhol—small, frail, and pale almost to the point of transparency—is certainly a study in contrasts. "He was a peculiar fellow by any standard," says Ferguson, "but he was an amazing draftsman. He produced drawings endlessly and at great speed. They were

impressive." Poorly educated, with below-average language skills, Warhol did not meet his academic requirements. At the end of his first year, he was denied readmission, one of many students rejected to make room for the burgeoning numbers of GI Bill students entering the system. But the teachers, aware that Warhol was gifted, rebelled and insisted that he be reinstated. Warhol not only returned but was given a show of his drawings. Ferguson recalls one day when Warhol walked into a classroom and announced, "Eventually you will all have a half hour of light." Warhol later refined that to "fifteen minutes of fame," his most famous utterance.

While in college, Ferguson met Gertrude Elsie Houston, a beautiful, shy, young woman with a literary bent. Gertrude came from a proud, hardy, farming family in Greene County, Pennsylvania. The Houstons' farm had been founded in the early 1800s, and though the family fortune waxed and waned through the generations, they held on doggedly. Gertrude's frugal parents had weathered the depression, but although the hard-scrabble farm was self-sustaining, it was barely profitable. Nonetheless, they managed to put all four of their children (one boy and three girls) through college.

(top left)
Ken Ferguson overlooking Sendai town, 1953

(top right)
Wesley Mills, 1970

(bottom)
Charles Harder, 1956

(opposite)
Kenneth and Gertrude Ferguson, 1954

Ken and Gertrude married on March 1, 1952, in Clairton, while both were still students. (Another one of the smartest things he did in his life.) They had little time to establish their marriage because shortly after Ferguson graduated, he was drafted into the U.S. Army. "I have always been a lucky man," Ferguson insists. "Timing, in ways both big and small, has always worked to my advantage. I was standing in a line of draftees being sent to Korea, when "Buttons" Lamendola from my hometown passed by, recognized me, and had me moved to the group going to Japan." There he served for eighteen months as a draftsman in the Signal Corps. For Ferguson, who had never traveled further afield than Chicago, Japan was an aesthetic revelation. He was astounded by the refinement of Japanese culture and immersed himself in the country's arts: architecture, gardens, and wood-block printing. Except for their ceramics, which he shyly admits he barely noticed.

When he returned from Japan in 1954, Ferguson worked at a stained-glass studio but found the work dull and uncreative. Cashing in a portion of his GI Bill, he returned to his alma mater to earn a teacher's certificate in art education. Gertrude suggested that in order to complete his course requirements, he take pottery classes at Carnegie Tech with ceramist Wesley Mills. By the second lesson Ferguson was hooked on clay but had little time to pursue his newfound passion. He graduated in 1955 and was hired to teach art in the public school system in nearby Sewickley.

Ironically Ferguson, who is today revered as one of the most successful ceramic educators in America, loathed teaching at elementary and high school levels. There were bright spots during this brief tenure in art education—his interest in ceramics continued, and the Fergusons' first child, Russell Lee Ferguson, was born—but Ferguson was desperate to escape teaching. He confided in Mills, who suggested that he attend Alfred University and study ceramics full time. Mills was on excellent terms with the head of ceramics at Alfred, Charles Harder. Mills had studied with Harder (though not at Alfred). On the basis of a call from Mills to his old teacher, Ferguson was admitted first to the summer school and then to the graduate class of 1956.

The New York State School of Clay-working and Ceramics was founded at Alfred University in 1900 by English immigrant Charles Fergus Binns (son of the co-managing director of the Royal Worcester Porcelain Works in England). Soon Alfred was placing its graduates in universities and art schools across America, dominating the nascent field of ceramics education. In turn this alumni network of "old boys" provided Alfred with new graduate students, many of whom were then also sent into the education system. This gave Alfred a great deal of power in the ceramics world.

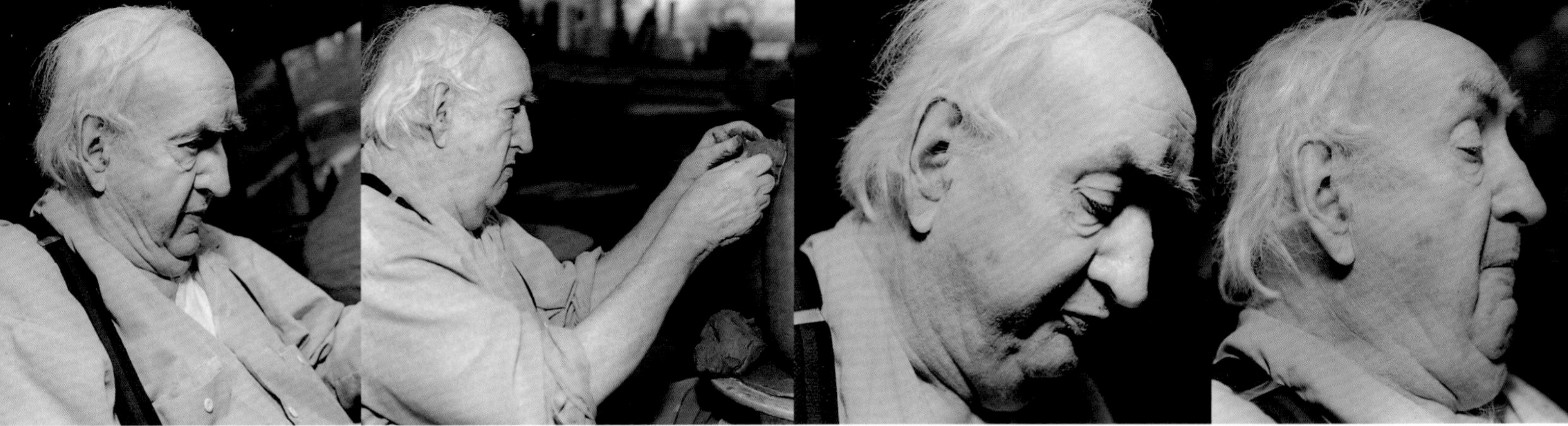

Alfred was then, and is still today, a hermetic institution, nestled in the verdant, wooded hills of western New York State. Situated in the poorest county in the state, the town of Alfred was small. The main street was just a few blocks in length and had one place to eat (a diner). It was also a "dry" town; no alcohol was allowed in public, although in private, drinking was the favorite antidote to the town's seclusion. The locals did not mix with the university folk, and the nearest significant city was Rochester, then more than a three-hour drive away. As a result, the ceramic students and the faculty were each other's sole company for the duration of their stay. This was not a hardship for Ferguson, who was now totally focused on pottery and appreciated being isolated from distractions.

Ferguson's teachers were Nate McMahon (a disciple of Bauhausler Marguerite Wildenhain), Val Cushing, Ted Randall, and Harder. Harder's health was in decline, debilitated by leukemia, and so his contact with students was sporadic. Ferguson had enormous respect for Harder, enjoyed his salty language and blue-collar pragmatism, and was awed by his deep knowledge of ceramic history. Harder, in turn, took to Ferguson, who embodied many of his teacher's qualities. Both Harder and Ferguson were blunt and pugnacious, called shots exactly as they saw them, and had an inbred protestant work ethic. They also could be touchingly poetic, particularly when dealing with the history of the ceramic medium.

Daniel Rhodes also taught at Alfred at the time, but Ferguson had no contact with him. He had been banished by Harder to the painting department; the two men had never seen eye to eye. During a lecture at a summer school, Harder showed a slide of a Tang horse and then announced, "There is more art in the ass end of this horse than there is in the entire Ceramic National in Syracuse." The reference was an affront to Rhodes, who had been one of the jurors at the event that year.

Ferguson had a great deal to learn in his two years at Alfred. He could not throw and admits, "I had no sense of form." He had no living potters for role models and did not know who Bernard Leach was, nor Hamada, Carlton Ball, or any of the other leading lights of the day. Many years later Ken would make the "pilgrimage" to Mashiko, Japan to meet Hamada. Indeed, there was no evidence even of nascent talent. All that Mills had promised Harder was that Ferguson would work hard and apply himself, and that he did. He would arrive at the wheel each day with a notebook filled with drawings of pots that he wanted to make from the night before. Then he would throw the shapes, quickly and repetitively. David Shaner, who was one year behind him, was fascinated by Ferguson's disinterest in making his pots more perfect. Intuitively Ferguson knew that throwing skills could be acquired easily. His driving energy at the wheel was dedicated to exploring the heart of all pottery—form.

A powerful man with immense energy, Ferguson enjoyed the physical release and exertion of this art form: lugging and preparing clay, throwing, and firing. In common with most of the graduates, he made the "Alfred vessel," a somewhat traditional vessel grounded in Asian aesthetics and functionalism. Although this approach came via Binns and his obsession with Sung dynasty ceramics, it also dovetailed with the Bernard Leach school, which was by then fairly well entrenched in parts of America. Also it should be remembered that Alfred's main role at that time was not producing studio potters but training designers for the tableware industry. However, the American ceramic industry was in decline, and Harder, a studio potter himself, recognized that there was a need for alternatives to factory-made wares. Hence, he encouraged those who wanted to become craftsman potters.

Ferguson eventually found his potter hero. Certainly Harder had this stature in Ferguson's life, but more as a teacher and scholar. Surprisingly, it was Kyllikki Salmenhaara, a woman and not a functional potter, who stirred Ferguson's imagination. Salmenhaara was one of the artists working at the ceramic studios of the Arabia ceramics factory in Helsinki, Finland (infamous for the infighting and jealousies of the participating artists). She had been a visiting artist at Alfred the year before he arrived. She left behind pots that mesmerized Ferguson. They were strong shapes with emphatic pedestal feet and arching necks. The surfaces were dry and rough, gouged with lines and texture, and covered in rich, color-saturated engobes that said more about the heat and passions of Tuscany than they did about her own cold native land. Years later Ferguson bought a pot of hers, a small jar, from an elegant furniture store in Seattle for the princely sum of $26. They did not meet until 1976 when she returned to teach again at Alfred.

Ferguson graduated in the spring of 1958 with an MFA and a solid foundation of pottery skills. His immediate concern was how to support himself and his family. Earning one's living just from making pottery was difficult, even more so at that time. Most of the better-known potters taught at schools and colleges. Academia had been the main patron for the ceramic arts in America for the first three-quarters of the twentieth century. Only in the last twenty-five years have galleries and collectors begun to rival (but not surpass) the power of the educational system.

Ken Ferguson (right) with Shoji Hamada (second from right) and Makoto Tashiro (left)
June 1973, Mashiko, Japan

Alfred had been a small, cozy world when Ferguson first turned up with wife and child for the summer school. Though the university remained a dominant force for several more decades, the ceramics field was about to explode. Art education, fueled largely by the GI Bill, became a postwar growth industry. It expanded dramatically through the early 1990s, and ceramics was a popular program in the new art departments. But given his unhappy experience in Sewickley, Ferguson did not want to go back into teaching.

The answer came from fellow potter, Jim McKinnell. He suggested Ferguson apply for the directorship of the Archie Bray Foundation, a potter's collaborative in Helena, Montana. The Bray Foundation was founded in 1951 by Archie Bray, with Peter Voulkos and Rudy Autio as the joint directors. It was situated on the grounds of Bray's brickyard, the Western Clay Manufacturing Company, which had been producing bricks since the late nineteenth century. The foundation was a haven for potters, a place where they could visit for short residencies. Voulkos and Autio had already left when Ferguson was accepted as director, arriving on June 11, 1958.

Ferguson soon had to face a series of crises. Archie Bray had died in 1953, and his son, Archie Bray Jr., had taken over. The business had fallen on hard times, and Archie Jr. lost the brickyard. He had built a massive tunnel kiln that could fire seventeen cars of brick a day, far more than they could ever sell. In addition, the five original beehive kilns were still operational. But the final nails in the Bray's brickyard coffin were that the clay mine that had produced a superb, brick clay since 1890 had run dry, and the new clay was inferior.

The pottery workshop was left with only $150 in its bank account. Ferguson then discovered that the foundation had never been legally registered and had no status at all. Luckily one of the students of the Bray Foundation's adult education classes, Jane Hibbard, was on the board of the bank handling the bankruptcy and assured the other board members that the workshop was a valuable asset to the town. The bank allowed Ferguson to stay, cautioning him that if the foundation were to shut down, it would likely lose any claim to its site at the brickyard. Ferguson managed to keep the foundation alive, if barely, by giving lessons and selling his pots and those of others (as many as two thousand a year), as well as by providing clay, glazes, and other materials and equipment to the small community of Montanan potters and hobbyists.

Pottery Studio of the Archie Bray Foundation, August 1978

PLATE 01

PLATE 02

The functioning brickyard was acquired by a rival company in Medicine Hat, Alberta, Canada, for $75,000. The aim of the purchase was to make sure that it never fired another brick. As part of the deal, the foundation was allowed to stay on, later acquiring the land that it occupied for $15,000. More recently, the foundation purchased the entire brickyard, a deal in which Ferguson played an active role. These twenty-five acres on the outskirts of town are currently being transformed into the largest ceramics workshop of its kind in America.

The closure of the Bray's brickyard was not the only challenge. Ferguson found that it was not easy to be an easterner in Montana. Voulkos and Autio were both Montana natives, and the interloper from Alfred University was viewed with great suspicion. "Hell, I even had a New York license plate on my car!" Ferguson jokes. But he understood their reserve. "People from outside Montana did not serve the state well," he acknowledges. "Montana had a history of having everything taken away from them, their gold, copper, cattle, and silver."

Filling the large shoes of "King Pete and Prince Rudy" was also daunting. Everything he did was compared unfavorably to the previous directors. It took years before these comparisons began to lessen, though they never quite disappeared. Ferguson was friendly with Voulkos but not close. He was put off by Voulkos's lifestyle. However, Voulkos left behind several clues as to his inspirations, including a couple of books on Greek pottery. The books, thumbed through so many times that the bindings were falling apart and the images were barely visible under the layers of smudged clay fingerprints, revealed an interest in the classical that underpinned most of Voulkos's vessels. Ferguson felt closer to Autio but looks back on their friendship as a lost opportunity, noting, "Rudy was working with bright, low-color glazes and earthenware, and I [was] too narrow then to appreciate what he was doing."

Given Ferguson's legendary bluntness, his work ethic, and his garrulous nature, the community eventually took to him—quite quickly by Montana standards. Soon gifts of wild game, beef, and lamb began to turn up on his doorstep, indicating that he had passed the community's informal residency test. He and Gertrude expanded their family; Charles Andrew Ferguson arrived on September 5, 1959, and Emily Ferguson arrived on January 15, 1962. There was a steady flow of potters through the workshop, David Shaner, Jim McKinnell, Fred Bauer, and others. But after a six-year battle to keep the kilns of the Bray Foundation firing, Ferguson was ready to move on. "I grew tired of working very hard so that other people could work," he recalls. "I wanted to focus on my own ceramics."

PLATE 03

PLATE 04

During his time at the Bray, Ferguson had grown less resistant to the idea of teaching but on two conditions: the position had to be in higher education but not a state or religious school. His timing was again serendipitous. In 1964, Dale Eldred, the head of sculpture at Kansas City Art Institute, issued an order: "Get me a potter." Eldred had a basic background in ceramics from A. J. Abernathy at the University of Michigan and Warren MacKenzie at the University of Minnesota. Ferguson was recommended for the job; Eldred approved. Ferguson moved to Kansas City and set up the ceramic facility. KCAI suited him perfectly. It was an art school, not a university, and the 330 students were mainly local. Within days he realized that he was going to enjoy teaching in higher education. "My students were so energetic and talented," he says, "I feared they would probably take my job away from me in a few years time."

Ferguson was never dethroned and stayed until his reluctant retirement in 1996. He set up one of the most important, if not *the* most important, undergraduate ceramics departments in America and ruled it with a firm hand. He developed the reputation of being a despot, a reputation that while not quite accurate served him well nonetheless. Tales of Ferguson hauling students off the wheel, frog-marching them to the entrance of the school, and bodily tossing them down the stairs and into the street were the stuff of ceramics-world legend. Of course, this never actually happened, and Ferguson's bark has always been worse than his bite. But for most, his bark—loud and resonant, combined with his ruthlessly accurate criticism—could be intimidating enough.

Ferguson's role as a pedagogue is described elsewhere in this volume, so I will comment only briefly on his teaching. He was a remarkably successful and effective teacher because, unlike many artists who teach only because they need the financial security, Ferguson thrived on his contact with his students. In turn, his list of students reads like the *Who's Who* of mid-career contemporary ceramic artists: Richard Carter, Andrea and John Gill, Chris Gustin, Richard Notkin, Chris Staley, Akio Takamori, Kurt Weiser, Arnie Zimmerman, and many, many others. They all emerged from his tutelage with a fierce desire to make art, an ambition to succeed in their careers, an understanding of the marketplace, and the valuable skill of photographing their own work. More importantly, none of their work looked anything like that of their mentor, perhaps the best compliment a teacher could receive.

The price that art teachers often pay in return for the stability of their monthly salaries is that their own creativity becomes secondary to that of their students. Ferguson was able to keep both tracks—maker and teacher—open and busy. Less than ten years into his tenure at KCAI, Ferguson began to question the direction of his own work. He was inspired by the growth and development of ceramics, which he witnessed first hand amongst his students. He was still making functional pots. "But I began to realize that it was becoming a cul de sac," he says. "I had got about as good as I was ever going to be in making mugs and jugs. I could make more, but I could not make them better. Bear in mind that most of us who came to ceramics shortly after 1950 did not set out to be functional potters. In common with Voulkos, Autio, and many others, I studied painting and meant to be an artist. But potters were not considered artists. I began to think about that, and I realized that I could not be both."

Ferguson had never liked decorating his pots. But in 1976 he began to draw on them. The motifs were inspired by many artists. Max Beckmann was one of the more influential, but he also enjoyed the clean, languid lines of Matisse, which had a simplicity that

PLATE 05

transferred well to clay. On a ceramic level, his pictorial influences came from the late medieval slipwares in the bountiful Burnap collection of English pottery at The Nelson-Atkins Museum of Art in Kansas City. In particular the Adam and Eve plates of the late 1600s and early 1700s caught his eye. They were drawn in slip and also painted on early tin-glazed pottery by unschooled potters. Both techniques required a deft, confident hand that forced an economy of detail. Drawing could not be labored, nor could it be erased and redone.

The result was a sensuality and vigor that entranced Ferguson and led to his own interpretation of the Adam and Eve subject matter, as well as his female nudes on plates, bowls, and vase forms. While he painted on the plates with a brush and oxides or slips, he also incised his drawings into the clay with a knife, a technique that also demanded brusque, decisive energy. This became his favorite way of drawing, twisting the knife to widen or narrow a line. Also, language began to appear on the work, lines from Yeats, Dunn, and other poets.

This brings up a personal side that illustrates Ferguson's spontaneity and generosity. I was giving a presentation with Margie Hughto at the combined NCECA/Supermud conference at Penn State on the exhibition *A Century of Ceramics in the United States, 1878–1978.* The exhibition was scheduled to open at the Everson Museum of Art the next year, prior to a national tour. When I left the podium, I found Ferguson waiting for me with a large plate. It contained a drawing of Eve offering Adam a pot instead of the apple, and inscribed around its edge was the legend "Adam and Eve and the first pot according to Garth Clark, 1978." "Good job," he muttered, "Your accent never slipped once." Then he pushed the plate into my arms and walked away. The plate is one of my treasures. It functions in my life as a kind of warrior shield, at once empowering me and guarding me from slings and arrows when I venture into the skeptical world of the fine arts to argue aesthetic equality for the potter. It sits in a place of honor at my desk in Long Island City, where I do most of my research.

Then in 1983, the rabbit arrived–more accurately, the hare or jack rabbit. It did not arrive through an interest in mythology, as some writers have claimed. Soon, Ferguson began to notice hares a-leaping all over the history of ceramics, from the slipwares of Spain to the porcelains of Japan. (Ferguson, in common with many of the best contemporary potters, is an avid ceramics historian, with vast knowledge of this sprawling field.) Certainly, the context of the rabbit's legendary virility was not lost on Ferguson. His rabbits, as taut and powerful as an arrow in flight, had the muscular thrust and aggression of male sexuality released.

Ferguson was no longer the polite, restrained formalist of previous years. His work was now often as bawdy as his language. His drawing skills were convincing and unlabored. They were not naïve but did have a certain freshness and innocence.

But he was unsure about this new direction. The fact that he sold the first of these works to a fellow artist, Adrian Saxe, encouraged him. His student Akio Takamori encouraged him to explore further by sending him a wonderful book of rabbit drawings taken from Japanese crafts, such as lacquer. Voulkos predicted that it would be an interesting journey, noting, "Ferguson's got this thing about rabbits and when Ferguson gets something, he runs with it."

Responses from KCAI to Ferguson's newly ambitious work were mixed. In part, there was political pressure for his work to reflect more contemporary issues. On the other hand, there were those who did not want ceramics to become too "uppity." There was an attitude at the Art Institute that ceramics was only a craft and had no place in the fine arts.

But the creative rabbit was out of the hat (literally and figuratively) and not about to return. Again, it was a matter of timing. Ferguson had spent twenty-five years in apprenticeship, learning about form, materials, processes, and manipulation of space. Now a little over fifty years of age, he was equipped with all the craft he could ever need and was ready to explore the art of his medium. His craftsmanship, no longer a matter of careful effort, had become almost subconscious. Ferguson could now allow the clay to grow and shape under his hands without the objective restraints of function and design.

His motivation did not come from a need to satisfy the school's demands, nor a desire to match his students or impress his peers. It came from a much more personal, urgent need within himself to take the leap into a new creative space, with the force and courage of the jack rabbits he observed at his summer home in Wyoming. He never looked back, and he succeeded royally. His work is now in the collections of art museums on five continents; his exhibition record is massive.

Few artists are so fortunate. Often at that moment in their lives when they enter their fifth decade, they are facing other challenges: loss of audience; flagging energy; work that is growing tired, too predictable, or too facile. For Ferguson, his life as an artist had, after a half-century journey of preparation, just begun. Good timing indeed.

"After so many years, he still is my teacher. I ask him questions and sometimes just ask for reassurance. He still gives me good advice, so I listen."
Akio Takamori

"Ferguson's got this thing about rabbits, and when Ferguson gets something, he runs with it."
Peter Voulkos[1]

KEN FERGUSON

The Palm at the End of the Mind

Thoughts of a Potter and Professor

PETER von ZIEGESAR

To get to Ken Ferguson's pottery studio, you take the old Shawnee Mission Parkway about twenty miles west out of Kansas City, past where the mission once stood. This was farm country, but the suburbs and subdivisions have grown up around it. Turn left and then left again, and go up a steep, wooded driveway that twists around sharply. If it's snowing, you'll be glad you brought your four-wheel drive vehicle. At the top of the driveway is the house that Ferguson built himself in 1970 after seeing Frank Lloyd Wright's 1935 modernist masterpiece *Fallingwater* in Western Pennsylvania, near where he grew up. The house looks a bit like a small suburban library: red bricks, one story, with narrow plate windows and a flat roof. Gertrude, Ferguson's wife of fifty years, greets you in the driveway with a bag of groceries and a kindly smile, and takes you inside.

At 76, Ferguson looks the same as ever, with a blue work shirt, open at the collar; a barrel chest; a high, domed, intelligent forehead; and large farmer hands that are crafty, delicate, and alive. Here, Ferguson sits in a pool of light at the dining room table, itself a modernist and utilitarian object, cut and planed from a felled tree that had grown near his old house in Grandview, Missouri.

You can see how much of this house is him: the clean lines; the plainspoken furniture; the shelves of hand-thrown plates and casseroles reaching up to the thick ceiling beams; the polished, unadorned concrete floor. Behind him are the shelf of art books and the stereo with selections by Duke Ellington, Jelly Roll Morton and Fats Waller, as well as a selection of classical music. To his left and his right are stacks of art books and correspondence waiting for his attention.

Ferguson, above all, has always been a practical man. His artistry grew out of his honest blue-collar need to make a living and to work with his hands. As his father made things out of steel, now Ferguson makes things out of clay. "What fascinated me about ceramics was the fact that you could take glaze calculations, work them out, and there would be an answer. I didn't have any definite answers before that. Something about that appealed to me; I don't know why.

"The broadness of being a potter also appealed to me. You build a kiln, and that includes welding and pipefitting. You mix glazes and clays, and that includes chemistry; you do some testing, you get some surprises. There is the physical thing of throwing around bags of clay. There's the physical therapy of working on the wheel. And still the

magic of working up a ball of clay and transforming it, quickly and easily, into something permanent, indestructible throughout the ages, and functional and beautiful. Plus, I've always been very much involved in the romance of firing a kiln, thinking of the old potters and the other countries you are introduced to when you start to study pottery: Korea, Japan, England, Greece."[2]

Gertrude brings two cups of Lapsang Souchong tea, and slips back into the chiaroscuro darkness. The air springs alive suddenly with the exotic, smoky fragrance. Gertrude and Ken's marriage has just such a redolent, pine-scented, aged-in-the-barrel tang. Originally a schoolteacher, Gertrude is an artist in her own right. A lush beauty in her youth, she remained an erotic inspiration for Ferguson throughout his life. This is evident in the thinly disguised nude self-portraits incised in his Adam and Eve plates. She also has a quiet, strong, deep, fine intelligence. She is able to anticipate his needs and keep his excesses within limits, such as keeping him polite when he needed to be.

(LEFT TO RIGHT)
PLATE 06, PLATE 07, PLATE 08

She does not like to speak about her role in his career—about other things, yes—but when this topic arises, she refers you to a statement she wrote for the magazine *The Studio Potter* more than a dozen years ago:

> We have had the traditional marriage in which husband earns and wife cares for the home. Male and female work roles today are not so clearly defined. Recently I heard an astronaut's wife say that while men give material support, the support they receive from women is a great gift; they receive the permission and freedom to explore, to discover, to become whatever suits them best, knowing that the women are caring for homes and families. That rationale is satisfactory up to a point: the freedom to develop an occupation that sustains one's interest for forty years is a fine gift, but so also is a family. Ken Ferguson explored, and discovered that he was an artist with a talent for working with clay, and another talent for working with people. But I cannot say that it was because of permission from me or anyone. One gives oneself permission. He had an extraordinary drive, energy and instinct. Nothing could stop him![3]

Ferguson has had one of the more remarkable careers in modern ceramics. As the salty, blustery chairman of the ceramics department at the Kansas City Art Institute for more than three decades, his influence on the profession has been enormous. His students have led the faculties of colleges around the country and helped to shape the cutting edge of the art form. Ferguson himself made a bold and surprising transition. He started out as a self-effacing studio potter in the mold of Warren MacKenzie and became an expressive and self-revealing ceramics artist whose work is shown frequently at the Garth Clark Gallery and is collected by museums around the world. Many *artists* take on the task of teaching grudgingly, as a day job, and end up giving their students the least of themselves. Just as many *art teachers* inspire their students while only feigning to keep their own gallery careers alive. Very few balance both professions so adroitly and downright zestfully as Ferguson has.

PLATE 09

PLATE 10

(TOP TO BOTTOM)
PLATE 11, PLATE 12

About Gertrude's part in his achievements, Ferguson adds, "Gertrude has great insight into people and things that I never really had time to think about because I was too busy with my job, teaching fifty art students at once. She would sit there, never saying a thing, but later I would find out she had been paying attention. She knew all about the students, and where they went, and what had happened to them, and what they were thinking."

Ferguson was born in rural Elwood, Indiana, and moved when he was nine to Clairton, Pennsylvania, a hardcore, blue-collar mill town that was the model for the film *The Deerhunter*. There, his father, Cecil, found a lifetime of work in a tinplate factory owned by U.S. Steel.

"My father didn't show much interest in my work as a potter," Ferguson recalls with regret. "To the end of his life, I don't believe he even thought I was doing that well. My wife made me understand that you don't change your parents. You just live with it and don't make a fuss because you're on your own anyway.

"Gertrude has helped me with that stuff. She's always understood things I didn't understand. So that's why you get married, because two heads are better than one."

Ferguson has always loved to build, and his first choice has always been to build with bricks. He has built salt kilns, gas-fired kilns, and wood kilns, and the house that surrounds us now is made of bricks. He recalls that the mill workers in Clairton used to carry large aluminum dinner pails to work whose oval bottoms were meant to hold soup or stew but were also just right for smuggling a ten-dollar firebrick out of the mill on the way home. If a worker managed to avoid the company cops, he would build a great big baking oven with the stolen bricks. Ferguson remembers his hometown dotted with these enormous baking ovens. So, one might say that the building of kilns was in his blood early on.

Barely out of high school, Ferguson worked in a tin mill, then a coke plant. As he tells it, "The typical remark you'd hear around Clairton was, 'I've been down in that mill for forty years, and what's good enough for me is good enough for my son, soon as he's old enough to get a job,' but Ferguson found that he disagreed. He began attending classes in painting and design at the Carnegie Institute of Technology and graduated in 1952, hoping to become a newspaper artist, and perhaps illustrate the sports pages.

The Korean War came along first. Ferguson was drafted, and through the chance intervention of a high school friend, was stationed in Japan as a draftsman, rather than being sent on to battle. Japanese architecture, with its clean lines and raw wood, opened his eyes to new ways of seeing. He spent his weekends touring, photographing, and buying up *Ukiyo-ye* woodblock prints, with their frank, practical depictions of bathing women.

On his return to Pittsburgh, he took a job designing stained-glass windows but quit after two weeks. Convinced he would be better off teaching in the public schools, he went back to Carnegie for a year of teacher-certification courses. One was a class in ceramics, taught by the potter Wesley Mills, who became a lifelong friend. "Within two weeks," Ferguson says, "I was hooked. I never looked back, and I never looked sideways."

Married and soon to be a father, Ferguson began thinking seriously about a career in pottery. Under the GI Bill, he enrolled at the New York State School of Clay-working and Ceramics (now the New York State College of Ceramics) at Alfred University, which was directed at the time by the legendary potter Charles Harder.

"I came to Alfred without much preparation," remembers Ferguson. "I could throw a pot, more or less, but I didn't know much about firing or glazes. Charlie Harder was an

outstanding teacher, a strong American who didn't see much point in studying anything that was going on in Europe. It was a tough two years, but I learned to think for myself and what I needed to be a potter on my own."

At Alfred he also came under the indirect influence of Kyllikki Salmenhaara, the famed Finnish potter and educator. She had left some of her pieces after her time as a visiting artist at Alfred. "She was my first hero," Ferguson admits. Salmenhaara made many of her modernist designs while employed by the Arabia factory, which would then copy her patterns and mass-produce them. The lines were classic—modernist yet functional—with a clean beauty that Ferguson successfully emulated in his work.

In 1958, with his Master's degree in hand, Ferguson took a job as director and studio potter-in-residence at the Archie Bray Foundation, an art center housed in a working brickyard in Helena, Montana. Although both the location and the foundation itself were fairly obscure, the job had a unique pedigree. Peter Voulkos and Rudy Autio had each held similar jobs there in the years preceding. "I had never been west of the Mississippi," Ferguson recalls, "and Gertrude had read all of the Zane Gray novels. It seemed a good way to get away from our families. We were excited to go."

At the Bray, Ferguson was consumed with the multiplicity of tasks needed to keep body and soul—and a working pottery studio—together. Russell Ferguson, his son, remembers trawling through the alleys of Helena with his father, looking for discarded packing crates in which to ship his pots.[4] Ferguson entered a vessel in the Syracuse Pottery Exposition and won first prize, as Voulkos had before him. He sold his wares at the Bray showroom and, because art supplies were scarce, began buying clay in bulk, breaking it down, and selling it along with other supplies.

Helena was isolated, but it was the state capital. As a result, Ferguson taught and befriended Montana's version of the wealthy and powerful during his night classes. They were homespun, self-educated, and eclectic people with whom he could trade ideas and from whom he could learn. He began to immerse himself in Japanese culture and pottery, showing slides of his travels through Japan and once projecting a copy of the classic Kurosawa film *Rashomon* to his friends. His pottery production was so great that Gertrude joked that he wanted to put a Ferguson in every kitchen in America.

It was during his six years in Montana that Ferguson first began to run into potters, such as Voulkos and Toshiko Takaezu, whose work pushed the boundaries of the simple, practical, kitchen-to-table pottery that he had learned at Alfred. Under this regimen, his trademark stoneware-baking dish lost its foot and became smooth like a bowl, with two worm handles and a fountain shaped lid. Practically speaking, this vessel was almost too large to be used as a casserole. This reflects an aspect of all of Ferguson's work: a matter of exaggerated scale. Ferguson is a big man, with powerful, rawboned shoulders; big hands; and a forceful, abrupt way of moving and speaking. The baking dishes and covered storage jars gradually moved toward a dimension that reflected his greater-than-average size and his gradually increasing confidence as a potter. His later work would expand on those proportions.

Ferguson takes you a few steps down the concrete pathway from the house to his free-standing studio, a small building crowded with the things he needs and uses to fuel his art. Ken isn't working today, so the studio seems unusually quiet, dusted with red clay. The walls and shelves flutter with postcards from all over the world, as well as knick-knacks, bottles, and notes from other potters. Scribbled out, you notice a few lines from T. S. Eliot's "The Love Song of J. Alfred Prufrock," which he long ago inscribed on a plate:

> I have heard the mermaids singing, each to each.
>
> I do not think that they will sing to me.[5]

"If you don't have things you love, that help you, give you a lift and comfort you, then you should go out and find them," Ferguson tells you. "That has worked for me all my life. Dan Rhodes said, 'If you love something, embrace it.' You can't love someone from a distance.

"My interests have exploded. I'm looking at all kinds of things. When I look at the pots, I still love them—English, Japanese, Korean. The architecture of Gaudi. And the paintings: Hieronymus Bosch; Matisse drawing a nude, seeing himself in a mirror; Picasso; da Vinci's *Deluge.*

WILL SING TO ME
T.S. ELLIOT
THE LOVE SONG OF
KPL
1-800-794-4780
MERMAIDS
I DO NOT THINK THAT THEY WILL SING TO ME
281-1000
GROUND SERVICE
SECOND DAY AIR
DAY AIR
70 LB LIMIT
130" (LENGTH + GIR
108" LIMIT ON L
FED EXPR
1-800 463
$126 LIMIT
WEIGHT
BRACKER'S
TOLL FREE: 1-888-822-1982
RECEIPT
Oct. 8, 1996
NEW YOR

PLATE 13

PLATE 14

"You must dig a deep well. It's my only quote. If you don't dig deep, it will dry up someday. You'll be 45 years old, a flash in the pan. An artist should have interest in everything but shouldn't be all over the place with his work."

Ferguson's long fingers pick open the pages of a book. "You ever seen this guy, Heinrich Kley?" he asks, and you look, and it's a line drawing of a crocodile skating with a nude woman. And with this image—sudden and rude, surprising and smart, and so typically Ferguson, whose gallery of interests ranges far and wide—our conversation starts to unfold.

In 1964, something happened that would alter the path of Ferguson's life forever. Dale Eldred, the recently appointed chairman of the sculpture department of the Kansas City Art Institute, was looking for a ceramics teacher to replace one who had left. Knowing very few people in the field, Eldred called Warren MacKenzie, an old friend in whose workshop he had once worked. MacKenzie recommended Ferguson for the job.

"I never knew why Eldred hired me, except that he was a big guy from Minnesota and was crazy about quantity and size. Archie Bray had had a railroad track spur going right into the yard, and sometimes the easiest way to ship clay there was by train. Well, when Dale heard I'd been using that much clay, he was impressed. I mean, here was a guy—talking about myself—who wasn't concerned about lifting a bag or two of clay; he was hauling it in by the boxcar!"

At that time, the Kansas City Art Institute was a place in flux, searching for its own identity. It was a genteel island of converted Italianate mansions, cool-green lawns, and impressive trees a stone's throw from The Nelson-Atkins Museum of Art and its collection of English and Asian ceramics. The school was not yet accredited and tuition was inexpensive. The student body consisted mainly of GI's out of Kansas and Nebraska,

Native Americans from Oklahoma, and guys who ran body shops and wanted to learn about art. "They were wild men with independent streaks," remembers Irv Tepper, one of Ferguson's first students at KCAI and now a nationally exhibited ceramics artist based in New York City. "I thought I was tough, but these guys were really tough."

Ferguson was not worried. If the school was unformed, he could better dig his own way into it. If the students were unruly, he could harness that energy. He quickly found a group of enthusiastic pupils and moved his operations into an unused carriage house. "It was a little-three-story-wooden deathtrap, with three big gas kilns on the bottom floor covered by a wooden shed [and] a narrow, winding stairway up the center," remembers Richard Notkin, a Montana-based ceramics artist who was one of Ferguson's earliest students. "We're lucky we survived."

In photographs of the time, he looks like a young Lyndon Johnson, lanky and informal, at ease in the sun, wearing a sun-squint, large hands and ears, a pointed nose, and lips pulled together in a discontented pout. He could spellbind his students with a throwing demonstration. His long sensitive fingers pulled the wet clay up into a tall cylinder as he told stories about his extended family, his sojourn in Japan in the army, Charlie Harder, Greek copper vessels, and Chinese Han dynasty pottery—peppering the monologue with his trademark raunchy jokes. One student remembers him as a cross between Bertrand Russell and Rodney Dangerfield.

Talented young ceramics artists like Notkin, Michael Peed, and Irv Tepper began to gravitate to the carriage house. They were attracted not only by Ferguson's passion for the medium but by his unifying vision of life and art brought together in the medium of pottery. The time was ripe for his message of simplicity, of returning to simple materials and utilitarian forms. His message coincided with the back-to-nature movements of the 1960s.

"To me it was more about a life than about clay," recalls Silvie Granatelli, a cofounder of the ceramics collective 16 Hands in Virginia. "It was about investing in yourself, and finding a way to express yourself in a kind of seamless life. It was not like you had art over here and a family over there. It was all one."

"Ken was a big, gruff man, sort of in-your-face," recalls Richard Hensley, also a nationally known potter and a part of the 16 Hands collective. "He was different than most teachers. He told so many stories and gave so much of himself. He had the self-confidence to know that just being around him *was* an education. He'd say, 'Come on, Rick!' and we'd pile into that beat-up truck of his and drive to pick up a pile of two-by-fours that someone had donated. On the way, we'd stop to get a hamburger. It was just his way of teaching—that just 'making things' wasn't all there is to art, you had to understand the flow of work, how to get ideas, and how to nurture yourself. He was teaching at all times. We'd be sitting at a red light and he would throw a line to me from a review he'd read about Jasper Johns. The flow of his mind was very impressive to a twenty-year-old."

Ferguson insisted all of his students call him "Mr. Ferguson" and learn the basics of throwing. However, he had the wisdom to let the exceptional ones, who were self-motivated and already working on a storehouse of ideas, have free rein.

"Nothing grows without freedom," he asserts, recalling those years. "If you're talking about kids at the Art Institute, most of them had talent. They just had to be inspired and get to the point where they really wanted to work hard. I mean they really had to want it bad. If they had those things, you couldn't stop them, really.

PLATE 15

PLATE 16

PLATE 17

PLATE 18

"I got so I could tell pretty quick. You take the sophomores, give them thirty-five pounds of red clay and say, 'This was your idea; you came to art school! Let's see what you can do with it.' If a student came back to me complaining, 'What am I supposed to make?' *that* would worry me. But if he punched the clay, threw it over his shoulder, and dropped it from the top of a ladder, I knew he'd be O.K. If he touched the clay well, then he had a chance.

"If a student was too tight, I tried to loosen him up. If he was too loose, I tried to tighten. And I tried to get them to try what was really unnatural for them while they were in school. The only path I encouraged was to start with the thrown pot. Start on the wheel and go from there. It doesn't hurt. But I didn't care if they stayed on the wheel."

On Ferguson's watch, the Kansas City Art Institute's ceramics department became an incubator where students learned the varied skills they needed to become working potters, from scrounging materials, building kilns, learning the chemistry of glazes and clay, and to dealing with galleries and art fairs. Reaching deep into history, he taught using the old model of a master and his apprentices. Students were expected to help build and fire the kilns and mix glazes and clay. When Ferguson was getting ready for a sale, the students were treated to the spectacle of their teacher frantically racing to put the necessary body of work together. It was a transparent situation, conducive to learning by osmosis. Later, students appreciated Ferguson's ability to let them enter his world.

The formula was: hard work and plenty of it. In the Indiana that Ferguson remembers from his youth, each farmer relied on an inner clock to tell him whether he had "earned his salt." That Protestant work ethic remained paramount. On hot summer nights, he took those still working out for ice cream in his beat-up carryall truck. Those who didn't put in the hours didn't get the invitation. He relied upon the students' keen sense of competition to keep them motivated.

"Yeah, he manipulated us in a way, but it was a talent that he had, and it served its purpose," remembers Kurt Weiser, an artist with the Garth Clark Gallery and a Regents' professor at Arizona State University. "He'd come over to where I was working and say, 'Hey, Weiser, you ought to see what Hensley's doing. It's unbelievable! Incredible!' Then he'd walk away shaking his head, saying, 'This Hensley guy is the best I ever saw.' So I'd think, 'What the Hell!' and I'd get up and sneak over to Hensley's station to have a look, and then I'd just have to work all the harder."

With Ferguson's guidance, students tried hard to instill in themselves a philosophy of non-attachment. Ferguson intentionally broke most of the pots he threw on the wheel, and he expected his students to do the same. There was a certain contemplative satisfaction and deep learning to be found in gazing down at your own vessels, smashed in the slaking barrels along with those of all the other students, remembers John Gill, who is now chair of the ceramics department at Alfred University in New York. "It added to your intuition. I spent hours memorizing the layers of history in the slop buckets, all that we'd tried to do and almost achieved and would try again."

The ceramics department became a haven for talented kids whose skills did not fit the conventional academic mold. Gill, who was dyslexic, had arrived at the Kansas City Art Institute literally unable to read or write. Stanley Welsh dropped out of Claremont High School in California because of attention deficit disorder (ADD). He began taking courses with Paul Soldner and soon found himself a freshman in Ferguson's ceramics department without a high school degree. Allan Winkler had been involved with street gangs

north of Chicago. Akio Takamori was serving a traditional pottery apprenticeship in the tiny village of Koishiwara, Japan, when Ferguson and Gertrude chanced onto him. By the following October, Takamori was a full-time student although his English was limited to a few swear words. For all of these students, and many more, Ferguson went to bat with the administration like a Big Ten college coach. He smoothed over missing transcripts, missed classes, and illegible papers making sure his students pulled the requisite credits to graduate while they spent most of their time working with clay.

While Ken Ferguson had certainly discovered his talent for finding and motivating students, his tenure at the Kansas City Art Institute also offered him stability and a time for experimentation. Working with wood-fire kilns and "garbage" firing, where the vessels were packed with bushels of leaves and other organic matter, he lost as many as a third of the vessels but was very pleased with the survivors. "I must live with the risks," he wrote then, "and be able to gamble with my work. At any rate, this is what my pots seem to be about, ... letting the clay and the fire show me something. Too much control would take the soul out of the pots."[6]

He fell into a schedule that was to work well for him for more than thirty years. He would work three days a week, from 8 A.M. to 6 P.M., at the ceramics department and spend the other fours days at his studio in Shawnee, Kansas, throwing. On Friday, he'd bisque his pottery, fire on Sunday, let them cool, and take the pots out of the kiln on Tuesday. "I didn't have the nervous temperament to sit and cut and fondle clay all day," he says. The varied routine, the student intrigues, the visits to The Nelson-Atkins Museum to gaze at English and Chinese ceramics made it possible for him to stay fresh, make pots, and push his work forward.

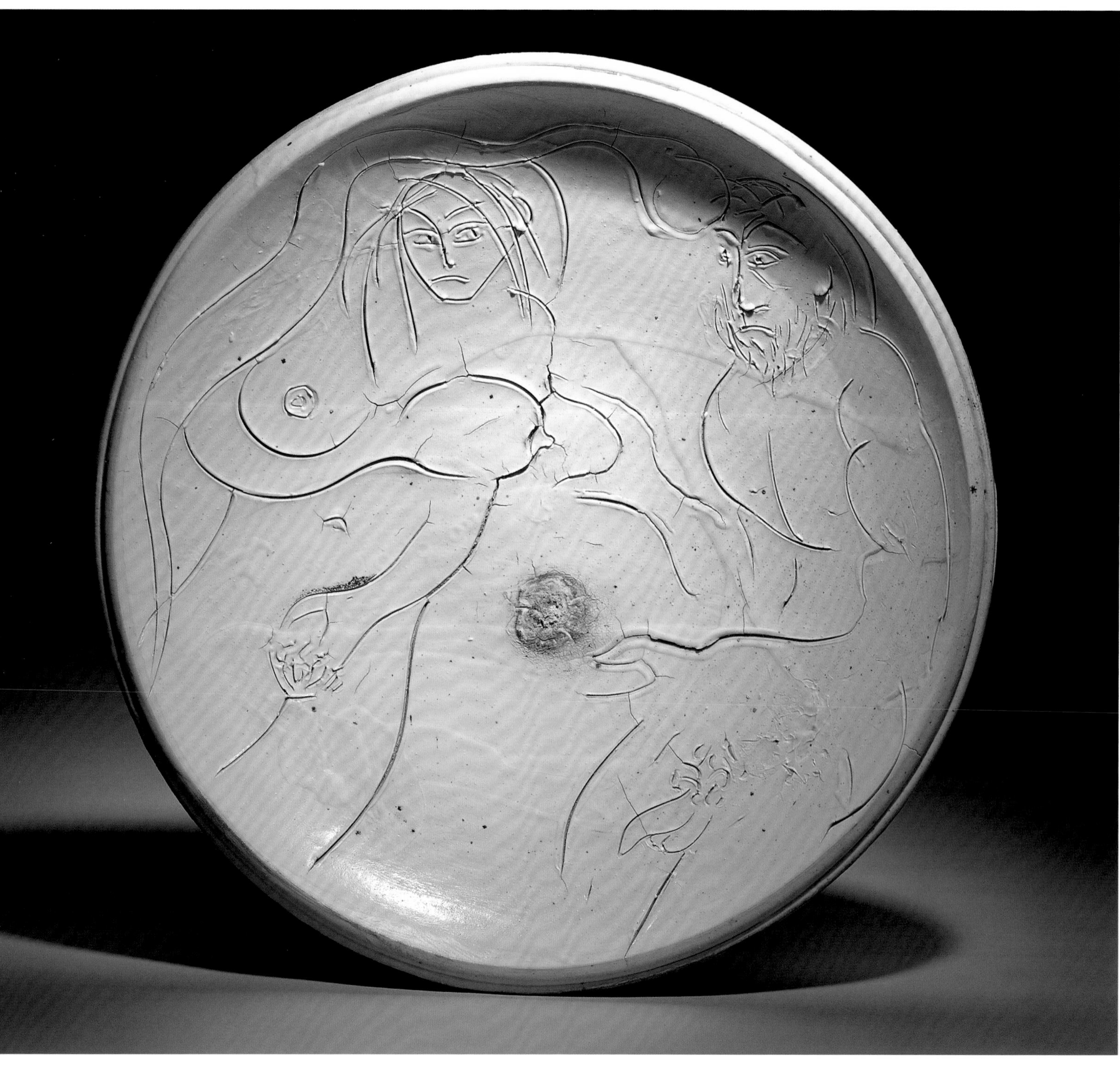

PLATE 19

In the next two years, Ferguson built a telephone-pole lodge and pottery studio on land he had purchased for a summer home in Wyoming. It was the first place that he and Gertrude had owned, and they marveled at the open land, the mountains, and forests. While his children went trout fishing with their grandfather Cecil, Ferguson could find space to dream and stretch. He noticed that the pots he made in Wyoming were different than those he made in Kansas City. They were looser, with more gesture in the throwing. His kick wheel moved more slowly than the powered wheel he used in Kansas, allowing for a slower, easier dialogue with the clay. The pots had more feeling in them; they were closer to Leach's ideal of "nonchalance," of having in a strange sense given birth to themselves, with the potter on the sidelines looking on. Sometimes a potter's greatest task is to recognize and appreciate the pot.

Having achieved tenure and feeling that he was "going to be around for a while," Ferguson also began to build his house and studio in Shawnee, Kansas. The decision was partly fueled by Ferguson's sense of competition with his friend and supporter at the school, Dale Eldred. He had just completed a modernist home nearby, a concrete bunker completely underground.

Improvising with little money, as he had at Archie Bray, Ferguson scrounged surplus timbers and borrowed workers from a construction site idled by a strike. Dale Watson, a local architect who had worked with Frank Lloyd Wright, helped design the home. It would be a modernist, one-story building, large enough to raise three children in. The utilitarian and sleek space would be like a Kyllikki Salmenhaara pot that you could live in. The hearth was the centerpiece of the building, like one of the enormous baking ovens the factory workers of Clairton had made for their wives from purloined firebricks, and was contained in its own sunken area off the living room.

Things were changing rapidly at the Kansas City Art Institute. By 1970, the carriage house had been torn down and replaced with a factory-like building. Its walls of raw concrete embodied more than a nod to Philadelphia architect Louis Kahn, whom Ferguson admired. Victor Babu from Alfred and George Timock of Cranbrook joined the faculty, two men whose two very different approaches to ceramics complemented Ferguson's.

Now the chairman of a vastly expanded ceramics department, Ferguson traveled around the country and the world—England, Spain, Finland, Japan, Alaska, Canada—recruiting new students. He would arrive at a college, show slides of Kansas sunflowers and Hamada pottery, give a pottery demonstration that would blow them all away, then tell a few stories and make a pitch. Ferguson's raw enthusiasm was catching and his salesmanship paid off. Students transferred in from other colleges at a rapid clip, forming as much as 60 percent of Ferguson's student body.

"Those were ripe years," Ferguson says of the early 1970s. Students remember that he ran the new department like a "great factory," with clay going in one end and pots emerging from the other. Jets of gas flame roared through the cracks in the firebrick kilns at all hours. The floors were open, with no dividers between students. Students were so self-motivated that they stood in line for clay and for glazes, and routinely worked twelve-hour days. The only way Ferguson could get some of them to go home at night was to lock the doors between midnight and 8 A.M.

A large figure, growing larger yearly, Ferguson maintained an outsize interest in, and sensitivity to, the inner lives of his students. For many, this close bond, forged of so many nights and weekends spent working side-by-side, did not diminish at graduation. In old Japan, the relationship between a master and his apprentice never ends. Ferguson's students tell of his reaching out years, even decades, later to help with a job, a contest, an application to graduate school, or just with personal advice. Many of his students received their first jobs through his intervention, in the years when a single phone call from Ferguson to a department head could make things happen. Married couples remember with a kind of awe that Ferguson pushed them together, or that when the crazy fragmentation of student life pulled them apart, he rejoiced when they got together again.

PLATE 20

Ferguson's personal, intrusive presence, his knobby prejudices, his loves and dislikes have always been out there for everyone to see. It was part of the Ferguson experience, the fecundity of knowing him. For students, he could be like the father you never knew or the one you were desperately trying to escape. For women, the locker-room jokes and Triassic level attitudes could be harsh, making their undergraduate years an ordeal of gritted teeth, of straining for a bar set a notch out of reach. Yet, Ferguson admired many woman potters. He showed over and over that he would help a woman student, the same as a man.

During most of the 1970s, Ferguson was content to view himself as a modest and self-reliant traditional potter. The idea of making simple, inexpensive, utilitarian vessels that could be used in any home, that were sturdy enough for the kitchen and beautiful enough to bring to the table, still had great appeal to Ferguson's blue-collar core. "My message was, I was glad not to be an artist. I was glad to be a potter. I was proud of this new thing we'd found, of making pots and selling them, teaching classes. I could build my own kiln, mix my own clay, and be my own boss."

PLATE 21

PLATE 22

But that role was beginning to show strains and cracks. A realist, he was not immune to the truth that American consumers reached for Tupperware when they wanted to store food, not hand-thrown artifacts. While temperamentally a populist, Ferguson knew his craft was not supported by the people he grew up with—the working class—but by a very small and rarified segment of the upper crust. Worse, the vessels themselves seemed to have reached a creative endpoint for him. "I started seeing that the pots weren't going to go much further." Ferguson recalls. "I had achieved a certain level of proficiency. My plates weren't cracking, and so on. I'd pretty much got my glazes to where I wanted them. With each fire cycle, I'd look at the pots and say, how can I do this better, where can I go from here?"

Clay is an ancient art. At first the changes in Ferguson's pots were evolutionary, for example, a fold in the belly of a wheel-thrown stoneware storage jar that looked like the fallen girdle of middle-aged flesh. Barbara Okun, who ran a gallery in St. Louis, saw this and encouraged Ferguson to make more. They evolved into his "slump" jars of the early 1980s: tall and expressively turned, upon whose streaming, brown rivers of glaze all the warts and wrinkles and sags of aging manhood could be seen on display. Large in scale, the slump pots had more than a little resemblance to, and some of the élan of, Voulkos's stack pots.

Ferguson wanted to push further, as Voulkos had done, but wasn't sure how much or how far. "I knew I was taking a big risk when I changed over from making pottery to art, truly," he says. "I was walking away from selling all of my functional work, without a doubt. Going over into the unknown. But then something happened. I had a sale in 1980 at which I sold $5,000 worth of pottery. That was a lot of money then. There were people in the back room of my studio trying to buy test pieces, and two women fighting over a cracked pot with glazes that had spilled all over, and I thought, 'They're not buying my pots, they're buying me.'"

At the wheel, Ferguson continued to wrestle with Zen ideas of "letting go, not letting go," allowing the spinning clay to occasionally twist under his fingers, hoping for the mistake or blinding flash of "nonchalance," that would propel him to the next level. Although he did not know it yet, the dam was about to burst and all of his creative energies were about to stream forth, leaping the old riverbed in a violent flood that would soon sweep all that was familiar and safe downstream and carve a new channel just as deep and steady.

But first, a personal crisis intervened. His father, Cecil Ferguson, was dying. Cecil had been the inspiration for all that was manly in Ken. Cecil had taught Ferguson about working hard, supporting a family, bringing home the bacon—and about not putting yourself ahead of any other man. Even in his seventies, Cecil had a bite to be reckoned with; he could give his son a thorough dressing down for not starting up a chainsaw fast enough. Cecil had never looked at Ken's pots, never encouraged his career.

Upon receiving news of his father's condition, Ferguson came to his bedside with a newly minted copy of Manson Kennedy's documentary film *Ferguson, the Potter* and a projector. He hoped at last to impress his father with all he had achieved and how well he was acknowledged. But it was too late. Cecil had no interest and waved the film away wearily. Soon after, he was gone.

Saddened by this loss, Ferguson went back to the studio and to teaching. Gradually, the changes he had been looking for in his work came to pass, not through a flash of inspiration, but by the laborious process of trying new things and letting his curiosity follow its own path.

The new imagery "started very simply," he remembers. "It was very straightforward and simple." He had begun by making high, looping handles in imitation of a ceramic basket he had brought back from Japan in 1973. He was attracted by the positive and negative spaces created, which reminded him of the paintings on Mimbres pottery. But the basket handles were more difficult to make than he had anticipated. He tried braiding coils of clay and rolling them out with a rolling pin. When he attached one end of the handle to a large baking dish, the other end would always come up short, or too high, or too long. Finally he hit upon the idea of joining two lengths of soft clay overhead with a quick pinch. The joint in the center gave the handle a pleasing, organic, sinewy look, almost like a piece of bone. But when he gave the handle two joints overhead, something astonishing happened: the handle looked like a loping rabbit. Ferguson then attached long, sensitive ears, hips, and a tail; the feet pushed out the rim of the bowl, creating an elliptical shape and thus—finally!—non-functional vessel.

The first of many "rabbit" vessels was fired black in a residual salt kiln; it was unique and simple, and seemed to express something essential about who Ken Ferguson was and what he wanted to say.

All of Ferguson's raunchy humor, as well as his historical learning, were channeled into his new vessels. A wrinkled, brown, highly sexualized, scrotal spout appeared on the front of a teapot and became another Ferguson trademark. He improvised on an ancient Chinese tripod form to make a witchy pouring vessel supported on a baggy udder, with a mermaid hag or mischievous rabbit peering over the handle. The rabbits begat more rabbits, marching around the rims of blistered, scabrous, green-patina'd vessels like bulls on the lid of a Han dynasty bronze. The rabbits leaped in twos and fours over each other and begat small, crawling, mute turtles. Although the output was less prolific than it had been with Ferguson's earlier pottery, in terms of creativity it far exceeded what he had done before.

As he had feared, with his first show of the "rabbit pots" at the Garth Clark Gallery in New York, he left many of his previous supporters behind. Even Warren MacKenzie, his old friend, was dismayed at the extravagance of the new work, asking, "What are you doing? What is this crazy stuff?" and perhaps echoing what Ferguson feared his own father might have said if he had lived.[8] But Ferguson's pieces were fetching gallery prices. Ferguson's canny Protestant character told him something must be right. A workman is worthy of his hire. It couldn't all be flim-flammery. Besides, as the famed ceramics artist Betty Woodman once joked to him, if it all went to hell, they still had the skills, they could go back to making teapots and casseroles.

What was the meaning of Ferguson's rabbits? Throughout world history and myth, the hare is a sly trickster, who seduces, bamboozles, and ensnares those who are less crafty than he is. In the pottery Ferguson admired, rabbits had an old and twining family tree, appearing in Mimbres bowls, English slipware of the eighteenth century, and ancient Japanese and Chinese ceramics. Without this historical pedigree, Ferguson probably could not have allowed himself to draw so deeply upon the hare's sinuous, muscular form.

But John Gill is convinced the rabbit is best seen as a self-portrait. "If you want to understand the rabbit plates, you have to go out to where Ken's studio is in Wyoming—it's bigger than life," he says. "There's so much sky, and you see a storm crack between here and the mountains, and then these animals running all over the place. There's something about the rabbit out there in Wyoming. It's not a bunny; it's this really great jack

rabbit. It's long and lean and *fast.* And have you seen pictures of Ferguson when he was at the Bray or at his wedding? He's long, he's lean, and *he's* fast. So, Ken's this rabbit. And he's saying, 'I'm just doing my thing out here. Give me the space I need.'"

Now in his eighth year of retirement, Ferguson stalks the pathway between his house and studio with a walker. Pain and a relentless procession of plans and thoughts keep him up half the night, and he is often unready to work until the middle of the afternoon. He works with the help of a studio assistant gleaned from the current crop of students from the Kansas City Art Institute ceramics department. Now it is under the direction of Cary Esser, who studied under Ferguson in the 1970s.

The rabbit has given way to the bull, another symbol of male power and sexual authority whose pedigree reaches back into ancient times and forward into ours—think of the Cretan Minotaur or Picasso's bulls. Ferguson's bull with golden horns (Freud would have a field day with this one!) on a wheeled, cast-bronze cart.

Ferguson keeps a voluminous correspondence with his former students, who still look to him for praise and support. If he doesn't hear from a student after a while, he will come looking for him or her. "Young people today are too cool to let on something meant anything to them," he says. "But you may get a letter ten years from now saying, 'You were right when you said that to me.'"

In his studio, Ferguson works on his calendar and sketches pots for his next show. There are twenty or thirty drawings to a page, the sketches so tiny and gestural that they look like Chinese calligraphy. He broods about many things, such as the fact that the human hand curves as though we still walked on them, as the first of us did. "I tell my students that they should think about this, because they are going to use their hands," he says. He also contemplates the Wallace Stevens poem that reads:

> The palm at the end of the mind,
> Beyond the last thought rises
> In the bronze décor,
>
> A gold-feathered bird
> Sings in the palm, without human meaning,
> Without human feeling, a foreign song.
>
> You know then that it is not the reason
> That makes us happy or unhappy.
> The bird sings. Its feathers shine.
>
> The palm stands at the edge of space.
> The wind moves slowly in the branches.
> The bird's fire-fangled feathers dangle down.[9]

Is that palm an exotic tree? Or the hand, which is the furthest limit and border of the mind's physical reach, the limit to our tactile senses?

"Ceramics has always been the low man on the totem pole," he says, in a voice as direct, flat and vigorous as the Indiana farm country from which he originally sprang. "We may have seen our best day—what do you think? Voulkos gone, Arneson gone, Viola Frey inactive. A Hamada teapot and a Matisse drawing are not the same thing." You look twice because you know that Ferguson loves Hamada, and he's saying something modest and direct about himself and his place in the pantheon of art history.

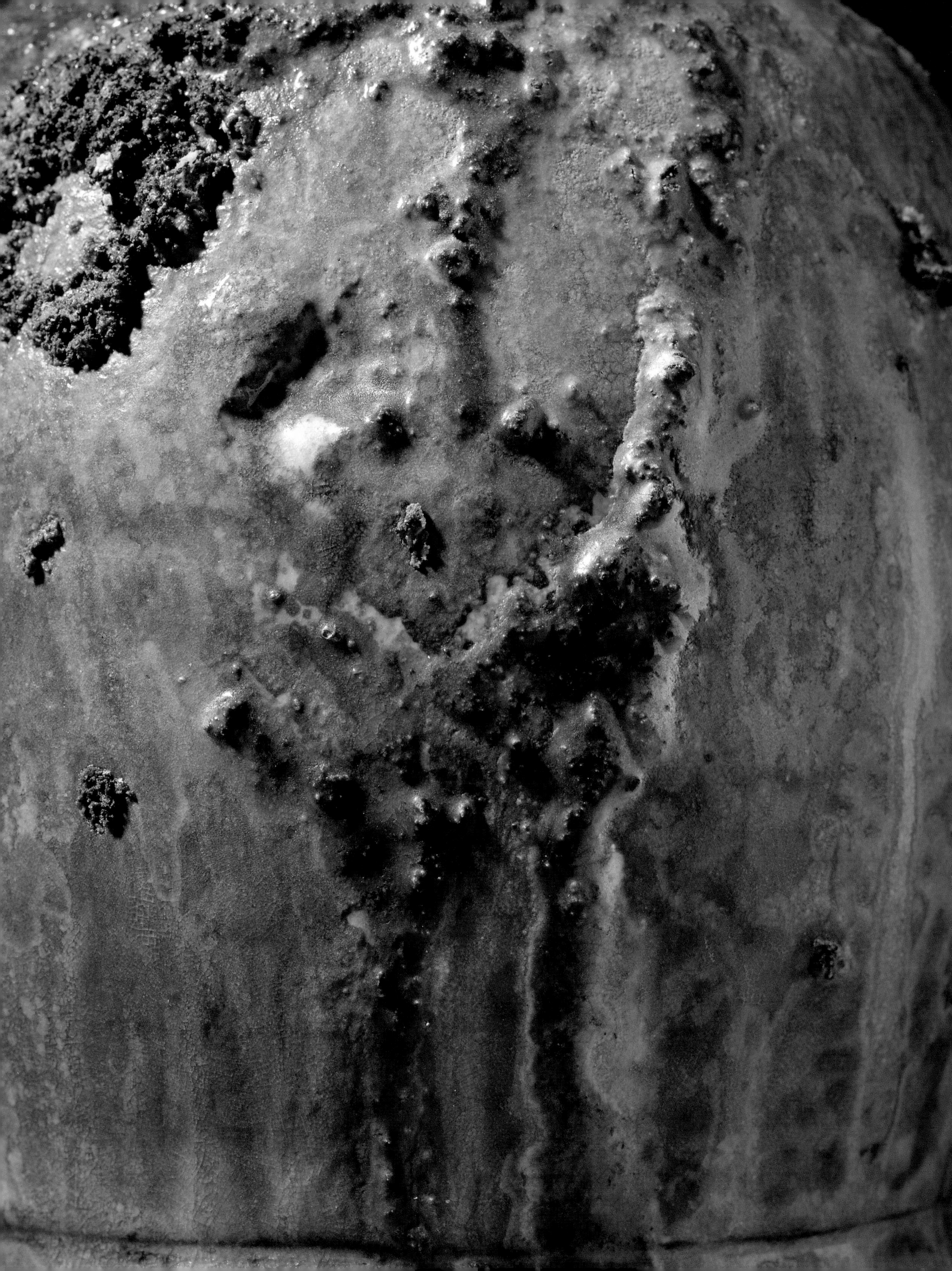

STUDIO CONVERSATIONS

TED ROWLAND

While Ken Ferguson is best known as a teacher, potter, and artist, many people tend to focus on his over-sized personality. Yet Ken is deeply aware that many decisions an artist makes are made alone in the studio.

On November 17, 2003, January 18, 2004, July 24 and 25, 2004, Ken shared his thoughts on studio life with Ted Rowland. The following interview is excerpted from those conversations

TR: You started out as a functional potter, and you are now known primarily as a sculptural potter. What prompted the shift?

KF: What made me change? It's not really clear to me. There wasn't a lightbulb that went off. It was about 1980. I was very productive at that time. Barbara Okun over in St. Louis wanted a show. She had told me a few times, sort of, like, stroking me and saying, "You're an artist," and all that sort of thing. I think all of us, when we started out in art school, we thought we would be artists someday. But I had been denying that for all my pottery career as a functional potter. I had almost been proud—"I'm not an artist; I'm a potter." And then we'd argue about artists/craftsmen and all these different things. I saw some other people doing things. They were breaking loose, and I thought, "I'm going to try that." I was a little bored making a functional pot. I was getting pretty good at them, at my pots. Barbara started talking to me, and I believed it. I guess I wanted to believe it, and I bought it. I slowly slipped away. At that first show, there were some platters with some figures drawn on them, some thin porcelain bowls, really very nice I think. So I made the switch.

The interesting thing is Barbara didn't buy anything out of the first show. I wondered about that. I had another show at the Morgan Gallery with Victor Babu and George Timock. Barbara and her husband drove over, looked at that show, and bought a pot. I asked her when she came out to the house why she waited to buy a pot from another show. She said, "I wanted to know if you really believed me. I didn't know if you really bought this. But it looks like you have."

Very soon after that, playing around here one day—trying to put a handle on a bowl, make a basket—I squeezed around, and I had sort of a rabbit. Gertrude looked at it and she said, "Is that a rabbit that's a handle, or is that a handle that's a rabbit?" Adrian Saxe got that pot, he liked that pot, and he still has it. That was the beginning.

Your work tends to be large, oversize, and heavy. What is the role of scale in your work?

I don't think my work is big enough. If I regret anything that I have done, I think I should have made a bigger studio and I should have made bigger pots. I'm a big man, and I can reach down into a three-foot pot. I can reach all the way down in there. Up until the time I was about sixty-five, I had a lot of energy. You're right; they probably are a little bit heavy. It's because it's black clay. I don't want it to sag and slump and melt.

Critics have referred to your recent work as "linear." What is a linear pot?

A linear pot has implied volume using carefully composed complexes of lines. There are lines in the hare and the different animals that connect to the lines in the basket, that connect to the lines in the legs.

Your early pots were distinguished by their mass. What prompted this change?

I made a lot of quick sketches of the pots, little drawings. I thought, "Maybe this will be helpful. Instead of writing down a description, why don't I just draw it? I can draw it faster."

Then I noticed the drawings. Some of the pots that had three legs, I really didn't like those legs to be rounded and stumpy. I wanted them to be sharp and pointed like I drew them.

That was hard to do. I not only had to make them that way—make those legs very carefully—but make extra legs so that when I put them on, if one wasn't so good, I got rid of it. Then I had to make a fourth leg to put upside down and support the pot so that there wasn't so much weight on the legs that they twisted and bent. It got to be complex.

What makes a great pot?

That's hard to figure out. You start thinking form follows function, and then you think all kinds of things. With the thrown pot, it's that you just don't want static, deadly, dumb, unfeeling things. You just don't want mechanical, no matter if it looks like it's perfectly made. The pot has to look like the pot's coming from a pair of hands. That it has gesture and feeling.

That's very important. You don't have to hope that it has feeling. You put the feeling in it with your hands because you've thrown so much that you can do it. You have a feeling for it. You understand it. It's not accidental. Sometimes you feel like it's accidental, but I don't think it should be.

What is the role of experimentation in your work?

Certainly not enough. It's simply I was afraid to take chances. I was always afraid that my experimentation would be a failure and people would laugh. I never had confidence, and that's why I worked alone in my studio. Most of my life I worked in a studio all by myself.

I'm not testing glazes in every kiln. I'm a production-type person. I love to get it done, to get it made.

You draw heavily on historical work. What is the role of symbolism in your work?

I love historical reference. It's very important to me. I want to go back even further than most of the books want to take you. I want to go back to the first guy that picked up a piece of clay and pinched out a bowl. I'm intrigued, and I'm interested in all that. It's sort of permission, like: they did it; you can do it.

Why does an artist need permission?

I think it's part of that fear of failure and making mistakes. You know you have to make them, and you know you're going to make them. But it's sort of nice to know that someone else has tried it and it worked out. That they did it and they got away with it. It gives you confidence that maybe you can do it. I was raised by a mother who told me—I think my whole life was built on—"God will get you for that." I always expected the worst. I was happy when things didn't happen.

There are certain images—like the hare and the tortoise, the fox and the rabbit, Adam and Eve—that you keep coming back to. What attracts you to those images?

I think they are very interesting forms.

I would really like to have the patience to do more with Adam and Eve–the Eve out of Adam's rib, Eve and Adam getting along very well in the Garden of Eden, the first problem, and being driven out of the Garden of Eden. People have sent me Adam and Eve postcards for twenty years. They keep sending them to me. I think it's great.

The rabbit: I love the form. I don't have a thing for rabbits, really. I actually know a good bit about rabbits. I'm not a biologist; I'm not a scholar of those things—I like the form of a rabbit. And if you were here watching me, like all of my assistants, they'll tell you magic happens when I put the ears on the rabbit. They watch for a week, working on these pots and wondering what is going to happen here. This looks like nothing. And I put the ears on, and they all say, "Wow! That does it."

The fox is a beautiful animal. Kind of hard to sculpt in clay, a little harder than you would think.

Turtle. Can't mess around with a turtle. A turtle is a caricature of an animal anyway. A normal turtle looks like a comic strip. They just look weird. You know, a big round thing. So easy to tip over on his back. His head sticks out then comes back; the feet and everything. So they're sort of comical-looking things anyway. You can't mess with them; there's nowhere to go with them. They're already ridiculous.

And then, of course, the bull. You see a lot of bulls around Kansas City. Breeding bulls at stock shows, at the American Royal. There used to be a bull on top of a huge pedestal downtown. You'd see that Hereford bull no matter where you went.

I thought I knew bulls. My wife went in and took a bunch of pictures of a Black Angus at the stock show. I didn't know bulls. I really didn't know bulls like I needed to know bulls. And so I had to do a little more research. It's especially hard to work on the heads. It's different than you would think. And there's a lot of mythology about bulls.

The horse is also a great form; been overdone a bit. Right now, I'll just stick to the hare and the bull.

Taking a step back here—you touched on this earlier, but I want to ask specifically—what is the distinction between drawing inspiration from a historical piece and being derivative?

You've got to watch that business of getting too close to those pieces. Somebody said to me, "If you love something, embrace it. You never got anyplace with a woman trying to hug her from a distance." And he said, "Embrace it, and after a while, you'll let go."

I like to look at old things and just sort of wonder how they did it and why they did it. But being derivative? Of course I am. That's O.K.; that doesn't bother me. It's O.K. to love something that's not yours.

Over the years, you've revisited a number of your forms. You started off with the slump jars back in the late '70s and continued with them for close to thirty years. What prompts you to revisit a form?

I like to go back to those forms and improvise. I love jazz. That's what jazz is: Billie Holiday singing "Sugar" so many times that one day she changes a couple words or important phrasing. And people who are really into this, they'll say, "Well, do you have Billie's first recording?" or the third one, or the fifth one.

That's what we do with pottery, we improvise. We throw this sort of cylinder, and we play with it, and we see what we can do with it. For instance, I made this so-called slump jar in Wyoming in about '77. I didn't make it very big; it was actually only ten inches. And it got a pretty good treatment in the wood kiln. This was still at a time when if something had slumped and gotten that uneven, I would have trashed it. But some how or another I just thought, "Oh, well, just leave this alone. You got a lid that fits. Just see what happens."

I enjoyed this jar so much—this is a lovely jar—and I brought it down here to the studio once and looked at it. I almost never do a thing like that. So I'm looking at this jar one day, and I couldn't make that jar. I thought, "What was going on in Wyoming that day when I made it? How come I'm not making it again?"

It's simple. I realized I couldn't make it because I was making it too small. When I made it bigger, I could improvise, and I did things with it. I started making it bigger and bigger and bigger, until I got them up to three feet tall. Then it was a challenge, really a challenge, technically and physically. You're a nervous wreck when you're finished because it's ready to fall over, sag, or slump, and you have to save it. The clay wants to go one way, you want it to go another way, and you have to save it. You do everything you can sometimes. And you say it's cracked, and it's heavy, and this and this. Then you say, "Who cares! Who cares! Nobody's going to carry it around."

So you have to play. They say Louis Armstrong would play "West End Blues" every night in Chicago for a couple years. A man who really loved Louis Armstrong said, "He never played it the same way twice." That was true improvising–having enough nerve to be up there in front of a crowd and change some things right in front of them. Takes nerve. Courage. Hard, hard to do.

For the last fifteen years, you have worked primarily with a black clay and a green glaze. What is the origin of the combination, and why does it continue to hold your interest?

I wanted to make a black clay. I don't know exactly why. I made this very complex black clay. People looked at the formula and said, "Never work. No good. Gonna melt. Gonna sag." But it's perfect. It's a wonderful clay to work with. I don't give the formula to anybody because they have a hard time getting all the materials, and then they blame me that it doesn't work for them.

I like that clay. I was making and firing pots that were residual salt. I had a salt kiln out here, and I liked the look of that black clay fired in a salt kiln where no salt was added. Just the salt that was in there. I got some nice pots. A little bit of a sheen. Nice things were happening.

Then I played around with a green slip. I wanted it to look like bronze. I wanted it to look like they dug it out of the Aegean Sea. And so I started making these bronze-like pots.

This is not new. This is old business because this is where pottery started from: the Chinese potter copying bronze pots. The bronze pots got there before the ceramic pots got there in China. They were melting down bronze and making bronze things with these molds. They lost the molds, they could only make one. Some even have some parts that were hammered out with a metal hammer on a rock. You can see, if you look in some really good books, you can see the first pots and the resemblance to the bronze. And these are, like, special pots—ceremonial, not just a pot for water or a pot to pickle some food. This was to make a really interesting vessel.

Your major source of inspiration is ancient Chinese bronzes. You've completed one work in bronze, at the Nature Center in Kansas City. Why not do more work in bronze?

In the early '70s, a lot of potters thought they would get a foundry and start casting bronze. Voulkos went into it in a big way. I would travel around and see their foundries, and I thought, "You don't need to think that just because you've got a foundry you're going to start making art. Your pots aren't going to translate into bronze; they aren't going to be that much better just because they're in bronze." I thought a lot of these people were misguided in this whole thing. It didn't work. I'm one of the guys that said, "This is ridiculous; I don't want to do that."

There's an awful lot to do with clay and a kiln.

Is control of all phases of the process important?

I'm not the person that keeps an exact schedule of the kiln, like what we did every fifteen minutes or every half hour.

I think you should know what's going to happen. I've had a few results with glazes that I couldn't repeat, and that is maddening. I remember firing a teapot that was just incredible, and I tried for two years to get that glaze to do that again.

Your green glaze has a variety of effects: it peels, it bubbles, it colors. Do you control the glaze?

There is control of this glaze. We have to oxidize the kiln toward the end. Get rid of all the reduction and fire it very clear and clean for the last half hour. It's supposed to make the glazes look richer. I don't know whether it does or not. Then we must fast cool this glaze for about half an hour once we turn off the kiln. My glaze, which is a slip, will crack and peel off the pot if it isn't fast cooled. Pete Pinell determined this firing sequence for me, and if I follow it I have success.

So, yes, we have some control. I know how I can get it to be brighter green; I know how I can get these bubbles and different colors; but still I don't want to have 100 percent control. When I open that kiln, I would like to see some things that I've never seen before.

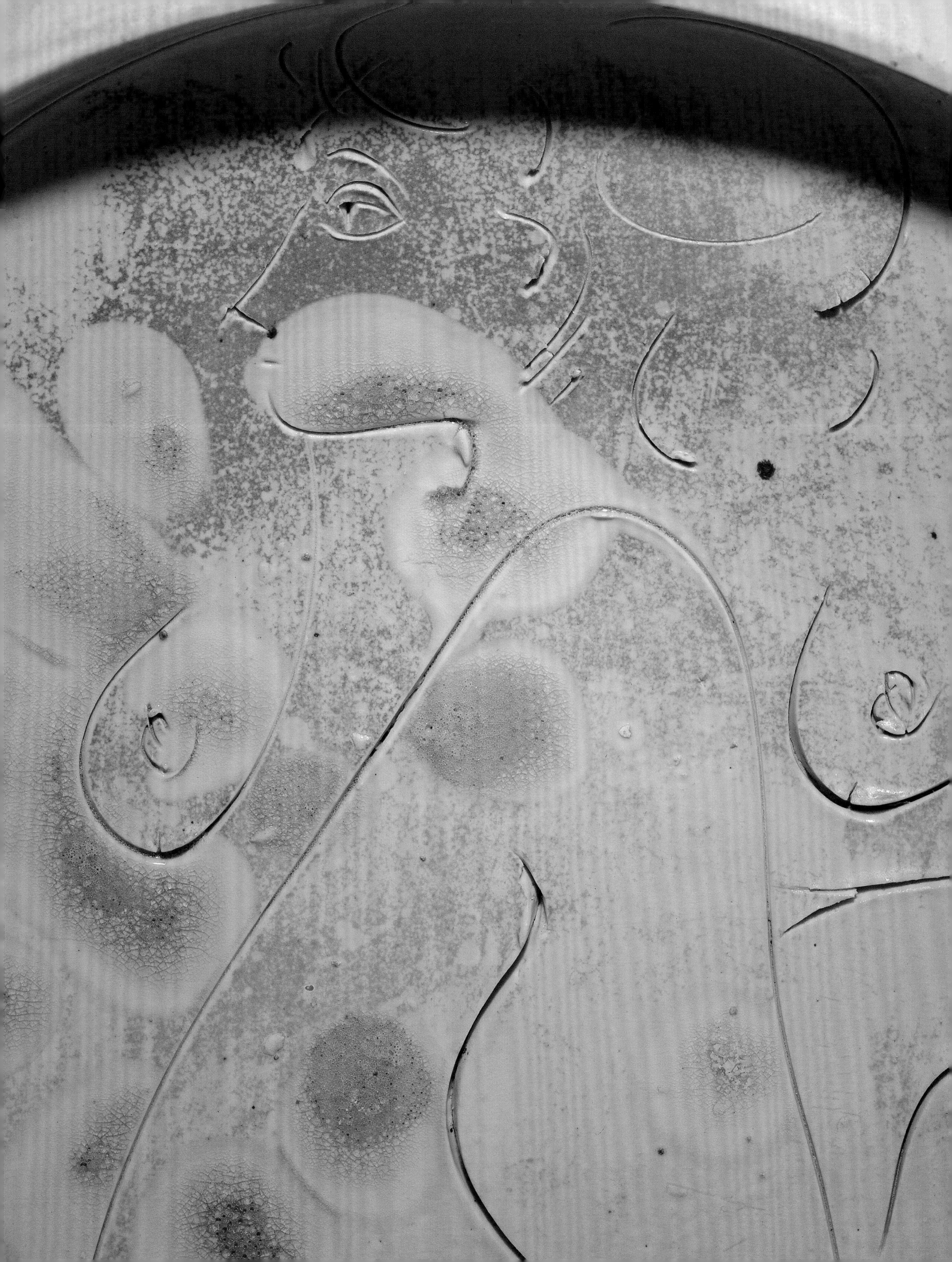

CLAY'S BODY
Ken Ferguson's Ceramic Art

JOHN PERREAULT

I: Introduction

What I propose is an evaluation and an appreciation of Ken Ferguson's remarkable ceramics, produced over the course of forty or so years. Ferguson is hardly unknown. He has exhibited widely and has had a retrospective at The Nelson-Atkins Museum of Art in Kansas City. He is justifiably represented in most surveys of American ceramics. And, of course, his students are legion. Yet if this evaluation is conducted properly, beyond confirmation of what appears to be a secure place in the history of ceramics, a certain education will accrue. All the strategies that an evaluation must employ will illuminate the artwork.

But isn't the perception of quality all that is required to evaluate and understand art? Isn't having taste enough? Otherwise-perfectly-sensible people will sometimes hold fast to the idea that taste is all—whether taste is educated or not—or, rather rudely, to the notion that the perception of quality cannot be explained.

I could certainly say that persons of taste will immediately perceive the quality of Ferguson's work and then leave the whole matter at that, thus clarifying nothing, elucidating nothing. I aim to be more meritocratic. An evaluation is about values. Ferguson's art works, it should soon be clear, embody values such as individualism, innovation, risk-taking, and dedication.

If I had to choose one art work to represent art made on earth, I would choose a vessel made of fired clay. I have said this before. The vessel is the pan-cultural form and clay very much the pan-cultural art material. How does a Ferguson rabbit pot reflect that heritage, add to that history? To understand his work, you must be familiar with the context.

We can of course try to apply painting and sculpture values to his ceramics. When he scratches graceful and impassioned drawings on plates, he can easily be related to the tradition of spear-headed drawing by Matisse and Picasso (and here we also think of Henry Varnum Poor). The iconography of the hare can be compared to Joseph Beuys's legendary performance *How to Explain Pictures to a Dead Hare* in which gold-faced, with a dead hare on his lap, this mystical/political artist did just that. The bronze hare sculptures of British artist Barry Flanagan also come to mind. But in terms of Ferguson, contemporary art notions of shocking innovation will never apply. Instead, he has pursued a steady course, more suitable to his medium, his milieu, his ethic.

PLATE 24

Is there a ceramics ethic? Most assuredly. I define the ceramics ethic as upholding the ideas of truth to clay, truth to process, and truth to form, but also as the commitment to heritage and depth of investigation. Ferguson is one of the major participants in this ethic. I see it expressed in his work over the years from functional pottery, through slump pots, to the investigation of rabbits and other animals. The teaching part of that participation I will leave to another essay in this book, but it is, no doubt, as clear as the work we can see and touch.

The ceramics ethic is the same as the ceramics aesthetic. This is why ceramics, although art, is different from several other art forms and traditions. Painting and sculpture, even in the prime years of formalism, made innovation, rather than individualism, the highest value and preferred appropriation over the kind of quotation and homage to historical forms, processes, and styles that is the ceramics norm.

The criteria for a fair evaluation of particular artworks can be determined in part by the artist's intended viewership and the values that are paramount within that particular context, by the operative historical context, and by the aesthetic placement of the work.

Ferguson's exhibition history and the work itself (in terms of material and process) leads one to believe that his intended viewership context is not that which can be defined by the Whitney Museum of American Art, The Museum of Modern Art in New York, or the Gagosian galleries in New York, Los Angeles, or London and the patrons of same. Instead it has been earmarked for omnibus museums such as The Nelson-Atkins, ceramics galleries such as Garth Clark's, and—in the past, when functional pottery was involved—for pure craft venues and direct studio purchase. This viewership can be identified as having a particular sensitivity to and admiration for ceramics of a certain kind, particularly the cross-cultural ceramic vessel tradition. Within the context of this viewership, Ferguson is a master.

II: Beginnings

The Ferguson story can be summarized rather succinctly, though Edward Lebow's more colorful version also offers psychological insights. A brief synopsis of Ferguson's life might read: Born in 1928 to a hard-working family in Elwood, Indiana. Earned his BFA from the Carnegie Institute of Technology in Pittsburgh. Served in the army from 1952 until 1954. Then took classes to gain teaching credentials, including evening ceramics classes. Following an MFA from the New York State School of Clay-working and Ceramics at Alfred University, worked as studio manager and resident potter at the Archie Bray Foundation in Montana until 1964, when he began teaching at Kansas City Art Institute, eventually becoming head of the ceramics department. [1]

My bare-bones narrative conceals the artist's inner life. Perhaps I should factor in his inner conflict with his working class, puritanical background; years spent refining his skills through making production pottery; and the release from production with the move to full-time teaching, affording him the opportunity to develop a more personal style and a number of signature images.

If the truth be told, a similar tale can be told of many ceramists of Ferguson's generation and, in fact, of some down to the present. There is, however, at least one distinctive feature of the Ferguson saga: what are now considered his signature works, the rabbit pots, did not emerge until he was fifty-five.

Suffice it to say that for Ferguson, as for many budding worshippers at the altar of clay, the attraction to ceramics solved the family-generated conflict between art and livelihood and between the useful and the aesthetic. That drama, although societal, is internalized. However, even a factory-worker father or stay-at-home mother—or a tycoon, for that matter—can usually understand the value of a good handmade cup. The craft traditions give permission to make art. Self-expression and beauty are fine if you can keep the results in the kitchen and if the product makes it possible to drink coffee or tea, bake pies, or divvy up a casserole. It's when that pot is moved from the kitchen to the living room, from the oven to the pedestal, that puritanism strikes again.

According to a 1993 interview with writer Peter von Ziegesar, Ferguson admits that it wasn't until after the death in 1979 of his father, "a man who had embodied the working-class ethic that rejected any kind of ornamentation or conceit," that he felt free to experiment in clay and really move beyond the strictly practical vessel form. Studying traditional Staffordshire platters and Japanese prints helped, but as von Ziegesar writes, "Ferguson felt a recurring fear that his father might burst into his studio unexpectedly, shouting, 'What is this all about?' With his father gone, he could bury his hands in clay to begin anew."[2]

Another important factor is that this freedom, although late in arriving, probably could not have happened outside an academic context of financial security. This has been the general case since after World War II, when craft departments in art schools and universities proliferated, providing sustenance to countless artists.

Looking back, the move of individual artists from pottery to non-utilitarian vessel-making and then to sculpture of some sort is parallel to the general shift of ceramics from shops and fairs to that of galleries and the shift from self-sustaining studios to academia. Of course, these days most students, sometimes with only minimal knowledge of traditional ways of manipulating clay, start with high hopes of attaining acceptance of their work as sculpture by galleries, usually immediately upon completing their degree programs.

In any case, if one can have worthwhile ceramic art without a grounding in pottery-making, this is yet to be proved. There are by now, however, examples of ceramists moving from sculpture to pots, from ceremonial vessels to useful ones, but I suspect the numbers are small. There are also some examples of painters moving to ceramics: Joyce Kozloff (for a period of time), Joyce Robbins, and Peter Schlesinger are three that come to mind, but none of them is interested in producing utilitarian vessels.

Ferguson's progression from potter to ceramic artist is similar to many now fully established careers, with, of course, some variations. For some, factory work and design were alternatives to the production pottery path, two examples being Elsa Rady and Marek

Cecula. Unless one is blessed with a trust fund, the need to make a living is life's first concern. Pottery in the past, and even to some extent pottery today, holds out that promise. It is a lean living, but a living nonetheless.

As a critic and curator who has made a point of honoring the pottery tradition, I will not claim that the pottery-to-ceramic-art journey is eternal, exemplary, or inevitable. In some cases, such as Ferguson's, the development was worthwhile in terms of the work produced. Sometimes artists might better remain committed to throwing wonderful pots instead of producing mediocre vessels-about-vessels or, heaven help us, sculpture. Not everyone will prove as talented as Ferguson at both pottery and more outwardly symbolic adventures. The conflict between pottery and "ceramic art" is not about forms, audiences, or aesthetics but is a battle of ideologies.

PLATE 25

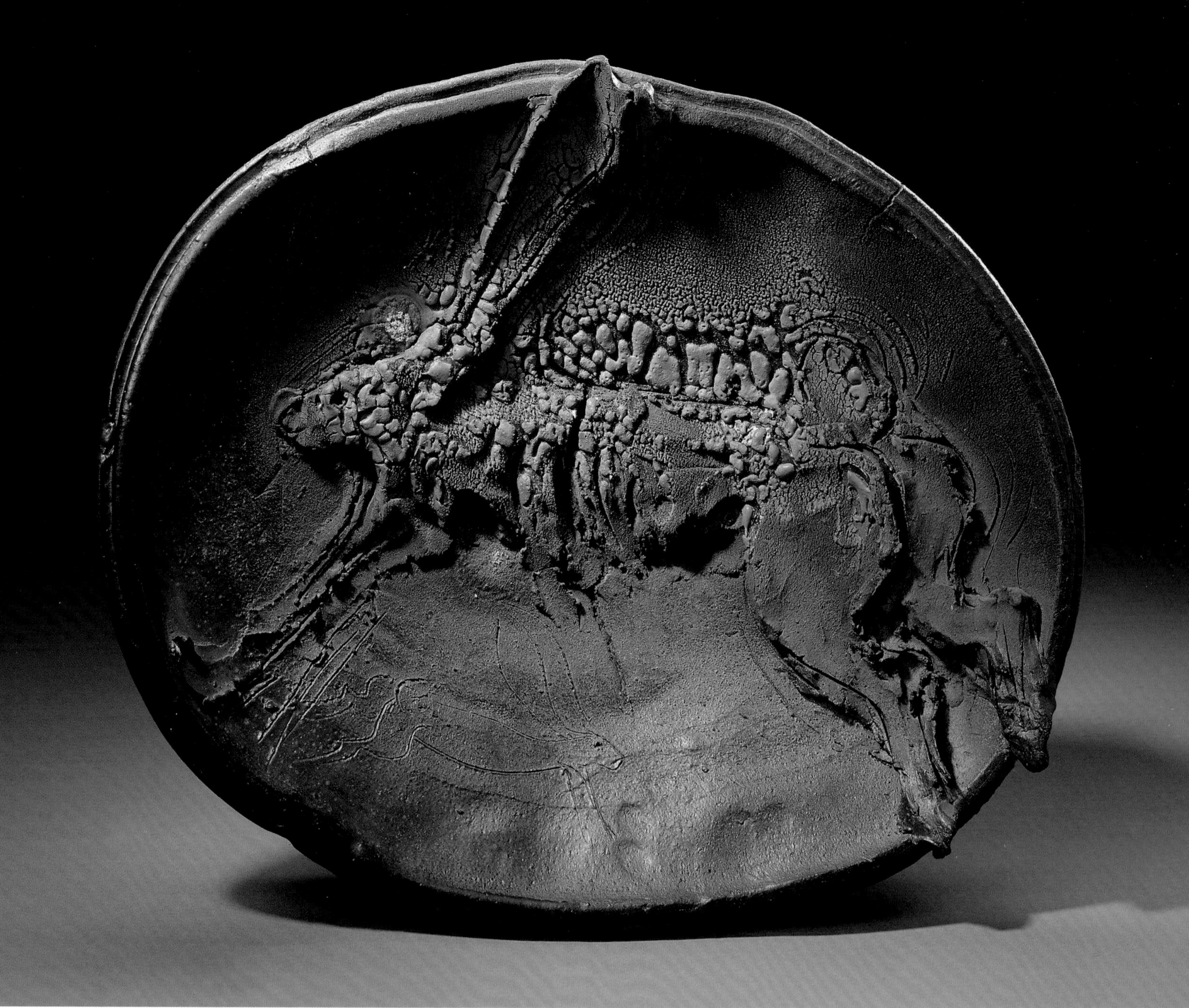

PLATE 26

III: Pottery

An evaluation of Ferguson's work cannot begin without a firm grasp of his pottery and the pottery tradition. One of the difficulties contemporary curators, critics, and artists of the painting and sculpture world have with ceramics is that the terms of reference are slightly different, and they cannot easily broker this adjacency. I am not sure it is entirely, as one curator stated publicly, that craft artists are not "playing the same game" as painters and sculptors—since beauty, meaning, and expression cross many genres—but that the forms, particularly vessels, are formally familiar, as are most of the genre and medium references.

The history of ceramics since World War II is different also, some would say off-hand. Instead of looking to France, as American painters did, ceramic artists primarily looked to Japan. The GI Bill allowed veterans to enroll in art schools in great numbers; fueled by what they had seen of Asian ceramics culture, and perhaps by Army crafts programs, some vets were drawn to clay. Arthur Baggs and British-born Charles Binns were no longer forces in ceramics. The nascent Beat Generation potters were not interested in Binns' refined Chinoiserie, but craved the trappings of Zen. Then along came Bernard Leach; his "master," pseudo-folk artist Shoji Hamada; and theoretician Soetsu Yanagi. All one has to do is look at the photo of Hamada, Leach, Rudy Autio, Peter Voulkos, and Yanagi at the Archie Bray Foundation in 1953 to grasp the impact of their evangelical tours. Peter Voulkos, who would be the hero of the next step in clay, is positively beaming. The Korean War, as in Ferguson's case, provided American soldiers with further Asian exposure.

For the most part, American potters ignored both traditional Southern pottery and Native American pottery. It would be strange indeed if this were merely because Leach had said that we had no national folk tradition. Perhaps in truth it was due to Beat Generation anti-Americanism or the idea that the exotic is always more attractive. Although Southern pottery has always had its connoisseurs, from the founding of Jugtown Pottery in North Carolina through the proliferation of face jugs and other roadside touristware down to the present, there has never been an American theory of the "folk" to match that of Yanagi.

That Americans looked to Japan and Korea is understandable, given our military presence there and the anti-Western thrust of postwar intelligentsia, but why British folk pottery was privileged is a mystery except, perhaps, for the persuasiveness of Leach himself and the British heritage of so many Americans. Leach himself was no humble, anonymous potter. But logic has very little to do with influence.

Here we must note how difficult it is to go back in time. There is so little documentary evidence of the vast amount of postwar pottery. Much of it, as was the fashion (à la Korean or Japanese folk pottery), was unsigned or signed with noms de céramiques. Then, too, it was ceramics made for use, so a great deal was broken or simply discarded, although sometimes flea markets will turn up prime examples, where, alas, identification may be problematic.

It is difficult to grasp how truly outstanding Ferguson's pottery is. One would need a huge survey of all casseroles (or cups or bowls) produced during the period by the likes of Robert Turner, Karen Karnes, Charles Harder (Ferguson's teacher at Alfred), Otto Heino, Warren MacKenzie, Daniel Rhodes, and so forth. Nevertheless, looking at reproductions from The Nelson-Atkins retrospective one can get a sense of the control the man developed. A storage jar from 1958, a decanter from 1959, a butter dish from 1961 (PLATE 02) all show neatly rising throwing rings, as do later works pictured here: a cookie jar from 1975 (PLATE 04), a batter bowl from 1977 (PLATE 05), and a casserole from 1980 (PLATE 10). The forms are serenely on-center. Of course, one cannot know a pot by an image alone. From an image one can get outline and some sense of glaze, perhaps even a glimpse of three-dimensionality, if the point-of-view is correctly angled. But you cannot get weight (and thus thickness or thinness of walls) or sound from a photograph.

Images can, however, ignite tactile possibilities. In terms of Ferguson's work, I remember the thrill of handling a 1962 storage jar in the collection of the Everson Museum of Art, where I was once senior curator. I also handled a 1968 raku jar from the Museum of Arts & Design (formerly the American Craft Museum), where later I also worked. Both have what we want from pottery, ancient or modern. They are graceful, yet solid. And in light of the pottery aesthetic of the '50s and most of the '60s, only someone with a really good eye and a really good feel for pottery would pick them out of a grouping of their contemporaries. Both "sit right." They neither look like inert lumps of matter nor as if they are about to teeter off their down-to-earth stance.

PLATE 27

PLATE 28

PLATE 29

PLATE 30

IV: The Body in Clay: Slump Pots and Wild Glaze

As we have already seen, pure pottery was Ferguson's first concern, and, like the studio clay movement itself, he eventually moved into the use of more relaxed, expressive forms. Perhaps this was through a more sophisticated understanding of Japanese traditions, but no doubt he was also under the influence of Peter Voulkos whose stacked pieces and slashed platters would have been difficult to ignore. In an essay for *The Studio Potter* in 1982, Ferguson wrote:

> I must live with the risks and be able to gamble with my work. At any rate, this is what my pots seem to be about—not all that controlled, letting the clay and the fire show me something. Too much control would take the soul out of the pots.[3]

But Ferguson, who had been incorporating glaze and kiln-generated "accidents" influenced by Asian traditions and their American descendents, was slow to handle the clay body itself more expressively. Not until the late '70s did he begin his "slump" pieces. Although Peter von Ziegesar, in an article for *American Ceramics*, ascribes this development to Ferguson's new body image as a man now in his fifties, with all the sags that flesh is heir to, I see such works being as much about clay as about flesh. Von Ziegesar also calls some of Ferguson's teapot spouts "preposterous, large, wrinkled, scrotal spouts." He finds Ferguson's artworks bigger than average and sees this as characteristic of his art. He describes this quality as "something in all of Ferguson's work: a matter of exaggerated scale," while drawing the parallel that "Ferguson himself is a big man with powerful, rawboned shoulders, big hands and a forceful, abrupt way of moving and speaking."[4]

I think von Ziegesar's description is in itself an exaggeration, but the relationship between the artist and his or her body—or more importantly his or her body image—is worth pursuing, bearing in mind that a small artist might also make large-scale works as compensation rather than as self-portraiture. Furthermore, scale is relative. Looking

(LEFT TO RIGHT)
PLATE 31, PLATE 32

PLATE 33

through the dimensions of the works reproduced in this book, I see nothing taller than twenty-seven inches. This is large, but not all that large. A typical Peter Voulkos "stack pot" from the '80s is over forty inches high (the "stacking" of thrown components was how he gained height). Dave the Potter, a nineteenth-century slave working in South Carolina, threw vessels five feet tall. Nevertheless, Ferguson's art "feels" bigger than most of the work around it.

Edward Lebow, an astute observer of ceramics, also finds the slump jars reflect the artist's middle-aged body:

> Their half-human scale—rarely longer than Ferguson's reach—gave them the physical casualness of an aging wrestler stepping out of a shower, or bellying up to a potter's wheel. These messy, towering shells of imperfection embodied what Leach had once termed "the natural limitations of both the material and the maker." They were the pots Ferguson had been wanting to make; pots, he says, "that look like me."[5]

There is, I suspect, some truth in all of this. The vessel form itself is body-oriented: literally, in terms of use traditions, and figuratively, because of ancient form analogies that afford very deep symbolic resonance. And although a more sophisticated approach to the body in clay than the above interpretations would have to qualify one-to-one relationships, this is an interpretive strategy that could well prove productive for ceramic-art critics in the future.

We still refer to specific parts of the vessel as the lip, mouth, shoulder, body, foot. The hollow is not only the voice but the womb. There are pot-bellied stoves (or there used to be), and middle-aged men in particular can have potbellies. It may be shocking to refer to some of the bases of Ferguson's teapot spouts as scrotal, but it is not irrelevant because wherever there is the body there is sex. And, to push the metaphor even further, wherever there is sex there is the great cosmic drama.

If the vessel is usually seen as female but Ferguson clearly makes the teapot spout phallic by the addition of scrotum-like junctures and supports to the spout, then the teapot becomes hermaphroditic. The 1991 Hare Handle Teapot (PLATE 28) is a clear example from Ferguson's later work, although the scrotal spout appeared years before the rabbit pots. The 1999 Tri-Udder Pouring Vessel with Mermaid (PLATE 45) turns bulbous tripodal feet that Ferguson has used before into three breasts. Ferguson's mythogeny is original as well as quotational or referential.

My thesis is that all ceramics of any importance is about the body, whether that body is the artist's or not. It usually starts out that way, since the artist's body, through the hands and the large muscles, is in direct contact with the material. As viewers sensitive to such content, we read the body of clay as our body. If Ferguson's bulges and scrotal spouts are autobiographical, which they may indeed be, this clarifies the body/clay connection in a way that no other ceramic art does.

It should also be stated that most sculpture is perceived in terms of the body of the viewer and the body in general. We identify with the forms, even when they are abstract. We dance when they dance, we repose, we jump, we battle, or we make love. Only Minimal Art consciously short-circuits this aesthetic pathway, substituting the Platonism of the industrial cube.

The ceramic vessel, whether or not it may be considered sculpture, partakes of this mechanism of empathy. Like sculpture, it is three-dimensional, and many of the same rules apply, until one needs to consider the circle and the sphere in their differences from either realistic bodies or rectangular abstractions.

Finally, to step even further away from traditional ceramics discourse, it is worthwhile to examine ceramics in general—and Ferguson's slump jars in particular—in terms of the Body Art of the '70s. Ironically, as part of the general disembodiment of art that was attempted after the disillusionment of the late '60s and the critique of dominant power structures in the art world as elsewhere, a number of artists began using their bodies as art works. Through Performance Art, women like Hannah Wilke, Ana Mendieta, Adrian Piper, and Eleanor Antin—to some degree building on the earlier work of Carolee Schneemann—their bodies to counter, confront, and critique the male gaze, societal debasement, and the art world itself. For men, such as Vito Acconci, Dennis Oppenheim, and Chris Burden, the male body could also be used as a last stand against the denial of vulnerability, the encroachment of false expectations, and the imposed confines of role or of gender. Except where photographic documentation of performances subsumed this new aesthetic, which it must be admitted it eventually did, the performing body was the art work.

I see ceramics as a form of Body Art, deeper and older. The thrown vessel, once fired, is like a three-dimensional photograph of the motion that created it and the body behind that movement. It is a document of the centripetal force. It is read as a body because it bears the earmarks of the body that produced it.

In Ferguson's middle period of experiments in firing, scale, and clay manipulation, it is evident that the looser ways of working yielded a new ability to go with the nature of the clay. Clay, that glorious mud, can be rolled and stretched; it can freeze in time and its own pliability, capturing the direction and speed of how it has been pulled and manipulated.

I am not claiming that Ferguson was directly influenced by Body Art, but simply that there is a correspondence that helps us to understand how his work developed from his early pottery to the slumped pieces and up to the rabbit pots. Of course, it would be helpful to look at the work of Peter Voulkos. The excellence of Ferguson's middle period, however, is that it expresses in a clear way the relationship of his ceramics (and therefore, I would claim, of ceramics in general) to the body and all the complexity that that kind of subject matter can generate.

PLATE 34

PLATE 35

PLATE 36

PLATE 37

PLATE 39

V: Platters

Ferguson has not only been concerned with the vessel, plain or fancy. Platters make up another large category of accomplishment. The imagery, whether inspired by English ware in The Nelson-Atkins Museum or by other sources (such as Max Beckmann), is traditional: female nudes, sometimes from live models; Adam and Eve; mermaids; and, of course, hares or rabbits. Most of his platters are circles, the oval being the most obvious exception.

Platters are the equivalent of tondos in painting and present similar formal challenges, although I suspect there have been more painted and drawn upon platters and dishes in the world than painted circular pieces of wood or stretched canvases. The circle seems to be more suited for the depiction of human and animal curves than for straight lines, since the frame edge is a curve that returns to itself. Nevertheless, adjusting forms to this shape is easier said than done. Ferguson, through natural talent and the study of historical examples, is a master of this format.

Formalism 101, as it were, dictates that shapes should in some way relate to or echo the shape of the presentation format. This does not only apply to the standard Western rectangle but to the tondo (and by extension the platter). For Ferguson this was both learned and instinctive, as the same applies in three dimensions when one is decorating a vessel or inscribing or brushing on an image or a decorative shape.

I need not detail how complicated such relationships of image or decoration to a rounded and an in-the-round surface can be. When an image or a pattern is unanchored to the presentation surface, whether flat or volumetric, I suspect most of us would detect a lack of integrity or, alternatively, a certain incongruity, although we might not immediately know exactly why. Forms that float in front of or break away from their ground are disturbing, or, if kept under control, stupidly trompe l'oeil.

Let us take three of Ferguson's platters as readable examples of his genius for inscribing the ceramic tondo. The following works are particularly suited to this purpose, since no obvious myth or subject matter intrudes (other than the mythos and the objectification/subjectification of the female nude)

White Nude of 1984 (PLATE 17) (salt-fired porcelain) is incised with gorgeous, quick and curvaceous lines that, since we are getting overlapping imagery, only slowly evolve into breasts with nipples, then a profile, then a buttock-to-ankle curve. Even a knee is sensuous. Here other arching lines become several different parts of the body. The blue spots that seem to have occurred by accident in the firing add further echoes.

Blue and White Nude from 1985 (PLATE 18) (porcelain) is more straightforward, with its brushed-on curves and elongated "Morse code" rim decoration. Nudes on platters cannot help but suggest flesh that is tasty enough to eat, and the formalism of the depiction (meaning the lucid relationship of the descriptive line to the encircling rim) reminds the viewer of flatness, conventions, and the play of the forms themselves against the literal representation. This contrast, paradoxically, heightens the joy.

Even more stylized is Ferguson's White Nude (1987) (PLATE 24) where the quick sgraffito lines sparsely delineate a prone nude seen from above, the genital area exposed dead center. The subject, her head pushed up the rim, seems to be looking down at herself, where ballooning thighs balance her delicate breasts. Surprisingly, the pose does not suggest the line drawings of Matisse. Ferguson figures out his own way to lock the figure to the surface.

PLATE 40

As fine and as engaging as his nudes are, Ferguson seems to have needed to add a layer of mythology to complicate his oeuvre. What better place to start than the story of Adam and Eve? Male as well as female nudes can come into play, plus a serpent now and then.

Adam and Eve Leaving the Garden (1981) (PLATE 14) is another salt-fired porcelain platter with cobalt "decorations." Their "leaving" Eden is really the expulsion; fig leafs have not yet appeared, but they are huddled together as if they know not much good is now about to happen. The delightfully executed brushwork snake—done in six swoops—seems to grin in triumph on the other half of the platter. The arch of the forlorn, guilty couple is perfectly balanced by the freely executed squiggle of the snake.

Porcelain Adam and Eve (1985) (PLATE 19) with its "Osage spot" like a dry wart is otherwise all sgraffito, depicting an unhappy, uncircumcised, bearded Adam on one side, a big-breasted Eve on the other. Just as in Adam and Eve Leaving the Garden, the ambiguity of affect saves the subject matter from banality. The exuberance and the efficiency of the

PLATE 41

scratched lines belie the frowns of the subjects, suggesting that Ferguson is on the side of the body. And although he seems to be making Eve's distended breast into the forbidden apple about to be grasped by Adam, the linear scratchings perform a lively dance against the continuum of the rim.

More stately is the Eve From Adam's Rib Platter (1998) (PLATE 41). Here the Osage spot is a sun, and Eve, like the other figures of God and Adam, is in partial relief, rising up with coiled hair that suggests dead snakes.

The mermaid is another Ferguson theme lifted from pottery traditions; we could call her the Kansas City Mermaid. Here it might be useful to compare two different versions: a sgraffito mermaid (Mermaid Platter, 1986) (PLATE 13) and a partial relief mermaid platter (PLATE 33) very much related in technique to the Adam's Rib Platter already mentioned. The former is much livelier, but the latter holds its own by the added dimension of the applied scales and hair. Both are vertical ovals and most suited to the mermaid configuration, or vice versa.

White Hare Platter (1982) (PLATE 16), Black Hare Platter (1990) (PLATE 26), and Shigaraki Platter (1993) (PLATE 30) all show Ferguson's favorite animal in relief, the first in salt-fired porcelain, the second in black stoneware, and the third a product of Shigaraki firing. All three are horizontal ovals allowing for the stretch of the running hare. In the first two examples, I like the irregularity of the oval and its rim. In White Hare Platter, the ears deform one part of the rim and, below, the hind foot crosses over it. In Black Hare Platter, both the ear and the foot protrude beyond it. The rabbit leaps from the platter into "our world." There goes formal containment, there goes restraint and good sense, which all seems to me like a brilliant way of showing that little beastie's trickster nature: the rabbit breaks the frame. In the Shigaraki Platter, although Herr Hare, Br'er Rabbit, Rabbit Boy, or Coney Island coney is safely encircled, he is shown mid-hop, kicking up his heels.

Finally, in regard to the platters, language also plays a part. Some platters are subtly inscribed with words running around their rims. One even presents a line from a W. B. Yeats poem about a mermaid. There is, of course, a tradition of words used in folk pottery: British and Southern American. Dave the Potter, the slave potter I have already mentioned, inscribed poems of his own composing on his gargantuan vessels. Here, as elsewhere, Ferguson pulls together another strand of ceramic history, making it his own.

PLATE 42

VI: Drawing on Clay

Ferguson's drawing talents have additional qualities, expressed particularly well by his fast, varied incisions into the wet clay. His drawings trap the movements of his hand and give permanency to the "thought" that drawing represents (drawing can be defined as the real-time expression of the speed, pressure, and directions of thought on a surface, using line). The sgraffito vivifies the materiality of the clay body—how moist or crumbly it may be, how giving or resistant, how smooth or rough. Erasure cannot be employed, and all hesitancy, stops and starts, endings and beginnings are forever captured.

It should be noted that Ferguson also draws on three-dimensional, rounded surfaces, and he takes this shape into account. In viewing the springing rabbits on Hare Handle Teapot (PLATE 28) and Fox and Hare Jar with Lid (PLATE 46), one is not sure if the thumbed-on or otherwise applied clay of the hare bodies came first, or if it particularized and gave low-relief substance to the scratched outlines afterwards. This ambiguity is part of their charm.

VII: Animal Tales

The hare or the rabbit is the animal most identified as Fergusonian, if there can be such a thing. I think there is. As we shall see, Ferguson makes tortoises, foxes, and even hulking bulls. But for the time being the rabbit or hare is his animal, his signature. No one else can use it; he owns it. And to give him his due, he owns it by virtue of his brilliant use of it as a form and as a symbol.

Where did Ferguson's rabbit come from? Lebow and von Ziegesar have both referred to Ferguson's rabbit as the trickster. But Ferguson denies he had the trickster in mind when he first discovered the form. He claims that the three-dimensional, lithe, long-eared hares he obviously loves to use are natural developments out of the ribbonlike handles for his "basket forms," or even chunkier handles, like that on the Basket with Braided Handle. The rabbits, like the handles themselves, sprang from the pliability of the clay. Ferguson relates that when his wife, Gertrude, saw his first rabbit-handled basket (PLATE 20), she famously asked, "Is that a handle becoming a rabbit or a rabbit becoming a handle?"[6]

Yes, he found the image of the hare on the traditional British pottery that he knew, but he also must have found it in the clay. The beautiful arch of some of the basket forms already suggested speed and some leaping animal bounding from rim to rim. Ferguson used the horizontal of the running rabbit to balance the vertical of the vessel form—whether teapot, tall basket, or jar. Alternatively he used it to reinforce the horizontality of flatter baskets or tureens.

The rabbit is a wonderful symbol, open to all, capable of inspiring multiple interpretations. If pressed, Ferguson will say that "the trickster is a fact." If you hunt rabbits, you know that the rabbit will circle back to where it started from and all you have to do is let the dogs do the running and wait. The rabbit diverts you from his warren. But upon his return, the trickster is tricked.

However, the real reason Ferguson began using the rabbit is because he wanted something organic. He repeats this several times. He also says about his use of animals in general that a book on Japanese design "gave him permission" to use animals in his art.

We all know rabbits are astoundingly fertile. We know what is meant by the phrase "multiplies like rabbits." We have already come across the theory that Ferguson was having a middle-aged man's forced reacquaintance with his body, as it were. After so-called scrotal teapot spout junctures, should the appearance of a live-wire, leaping hare be such a surprise?

Like the lion, the tiger, and the wolf, the rabbit is not female. Almost as if to balance the vessel/womb metaphor, Ferguson sometimes feels it is necessary to add to his scrotal teapots (as in Hare Handle Teapots of 1991 and 1995) (PLATES 28 AND 34) further masculine claims through ribbonlike, hare body-loops for handles. This is further proof that the hare with its elongated, leaping body serves formal, sculptural ends, as well as poetic, symbolic, and narrative themes.

PLATE 43

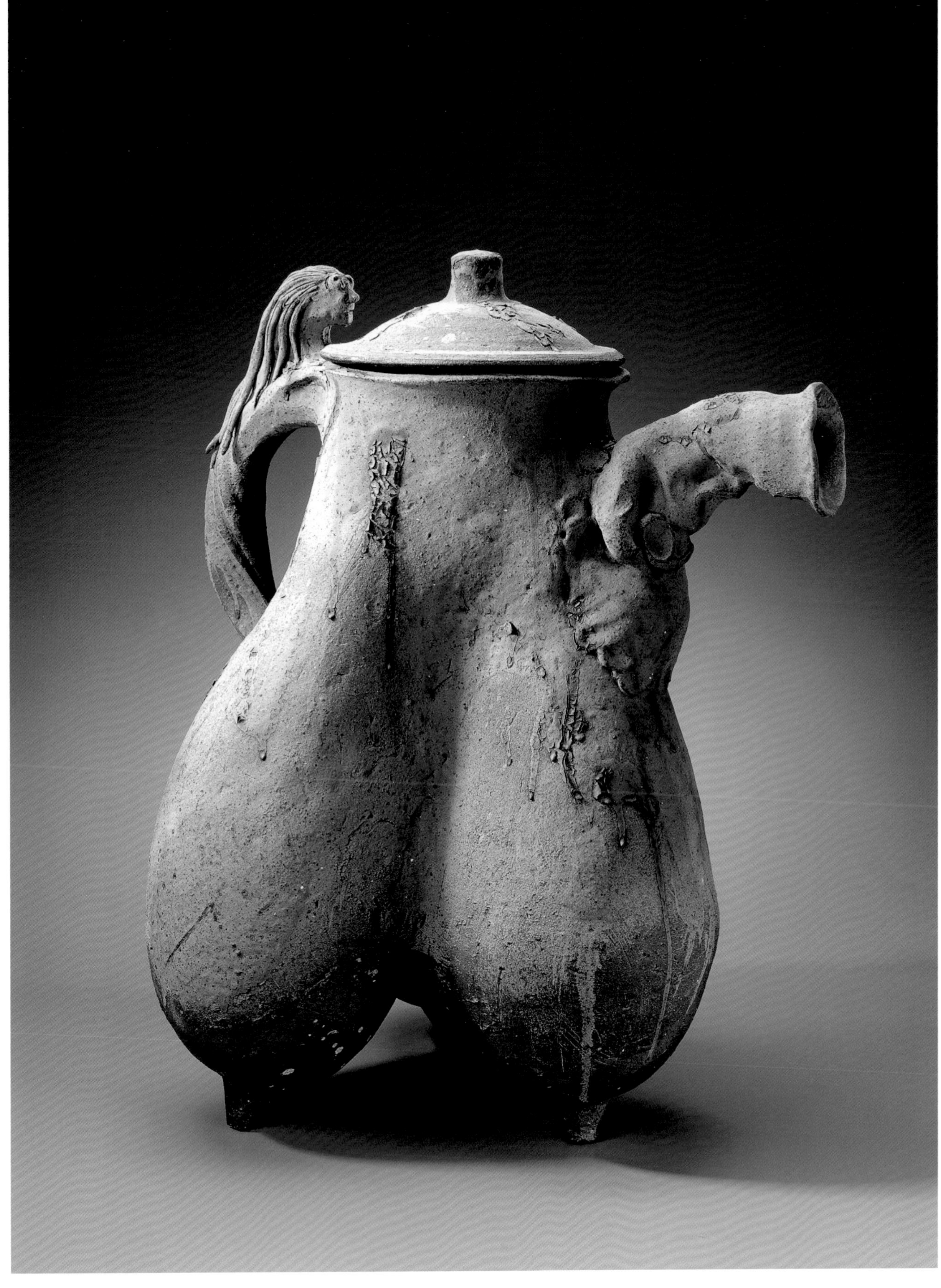

PLATE 45

PLATE 46

In at least one case, Four-Legged Hare Handle Basket (1997) (PLATE 37), the rabbit assumes a stubborn stance, his front and back legs firmly planted on the rim of the flattened basket form, his back is arched like a threatened or threatening tomcat. Four rabbit heads with ears flattened back adorn the four legs, suggesting adoration. Here, as elsewhere, the rough, varied kiln-wrought surfaces—crusty, pocked, and scorched—impart a patina of the ancient. One imagines a rabbit cult. Were the tender rabbit-liver offerings here flambéed? Or is the rabbit-god not Peter Rabbit, Br'er Rabbit, or Bugs Bunny but something decidedly less benign?

However, one should not let Ferguson's serious surfaces lead one to exclusively emphasize the gravitas of the rabbit. This large rodent is also a figure of delight—as long as it is not your personal cabbage patch he is after. In this regard, what could be more joyous than Leap Frog Hare Basket of 2001 (PLATE 47). What better proof than the enormous handles of this delightful basket that Ferguson's rabbits, like the hares in folklore, are human stand-ins or at least references to those talking hares. The two rabbits are almost free of the basket (i.e., vessel), for as a platter with two up-turned opposing sides, although it has considerable sculptural interest, it functions more as a base.

More recently, Rabbit Man breaks free—to become a tricycle. Hare on Wheels (Ears Flat) (PLATE 52) and Hare on Wheels (Ears Up) (PLATE 51), both 2003, are clay toys from some demonic nursery, emblems of a second childhood, perhaps. They marry menace and charm. The wheels are of cast bronze, the molds taken from small wheels thrown by Ferguson. He did not want them perfect and mechanical. Since discovering a book on ancient Hunan Chinese bronzes and then going on to study them in great detail, he has been influenced by the patinas—which is quite evident in the animal pots where he uses a black clay body—and thought he would like to work in bronze himself. The wheel itself, as befitting someone whose primary tool is the potter's wheel, is an obsession.

PLATE 47

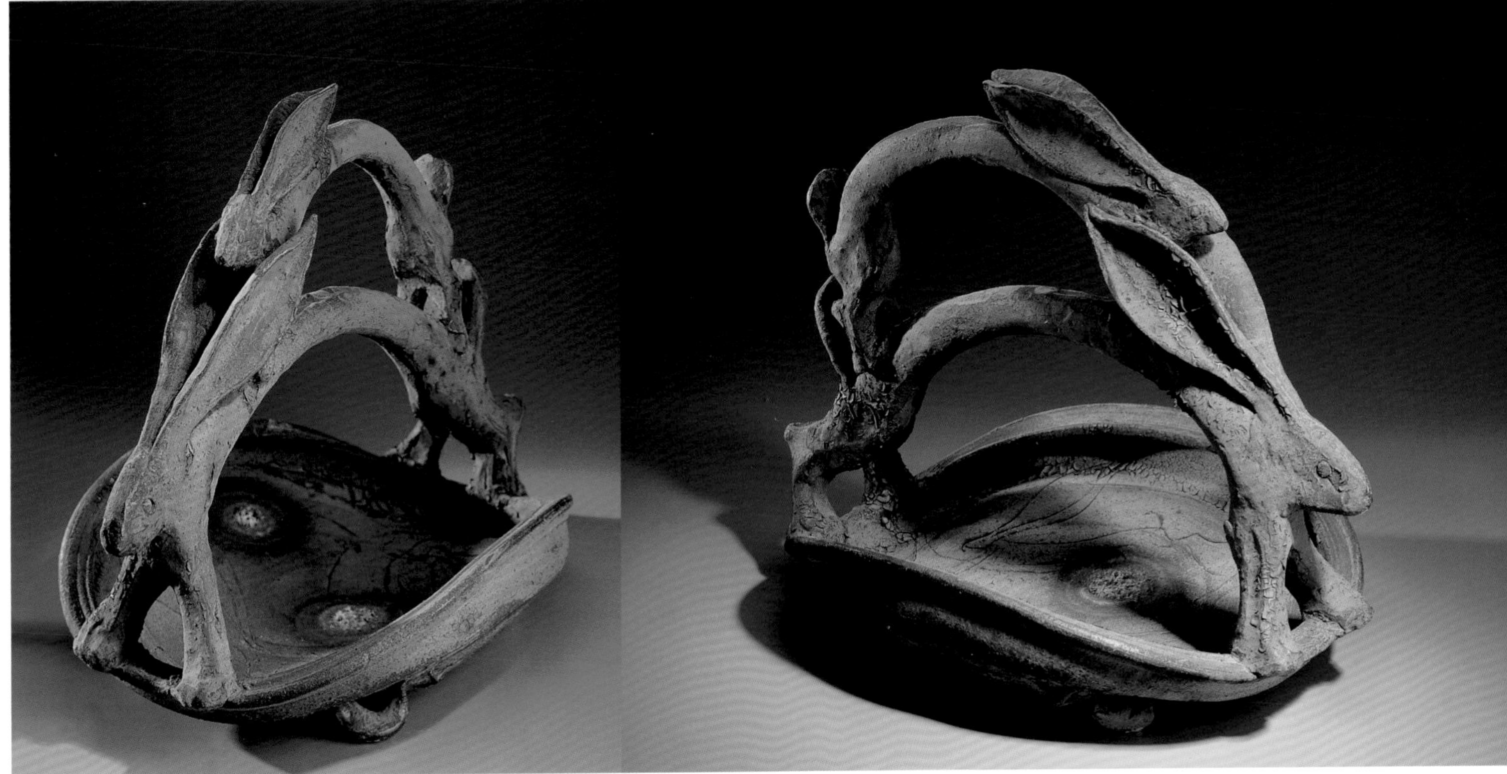

And what of the bulls-on-wheels? Black Clay Bull—Red Glaze (PLATE 48) and Black Bull on Bronze Cart (PLATE 54), (2002 and 2003, respectively) are daring indeed. Like the mermaid, the bull has been another Ferguson leitmotif, usually taking the form of a head alone or a full figure on a lid. How foursquare is Ferguson's bull; he (again, a male animal) is not transformed into a tricycle. Instead, chain through his nostrils, his horns lowered or on high, he is ready for admiration, pulled on a cart though town, as in some ancient public ceremony honoring his masculinity and strength. Is this the fierceness and the stubbornness of old age? The initial inspiration was the sight of Black Angus bulls in competition in Kansas City, once known for its stockyards, but the bull, like the hare, is what could be called a natural symbol.

The narratives continue. There are certain works that are more obviously storytelling. Anything with a tortoise and a hare, such as Four-legged Tureen with Lid (1996) (PLATE 35) and Tripod T-Pot (1999) (PLATE 44), has to recall Aesop's classical race. In fact, given the context, any work with more than one kind of animal (e.g. Fox and Hare Jar with Lid of 2000) will necessarily evoke a narrative feel, if not particular tales.

VIII: Narratives in Clay

Process is story. If the truth be told, even the most austere Sung porcelain has a tale to tell—and if a masterpiece, tells it well. The more visible the making of the ceramic artwork; the more encapsulated the process through throwing marks, clay manipulation, firings; the more self-evident the intended use; the more formally self-referential and the more referential to other ceramics (one object can do both)—well, then, the more like literature is this oldest of art forms. Narration at its best is poetry.

Thus, Ferguson in the development of his career—a story in itself—moves from restrained (and quite elegant) pottery, to more overt self-expression (the slump pots and wild glazes), to the animal tales. The pottery tells the story of its own making and use. The slump works tell the story of their making more overtly, abandoning use and factoring in the artist's own body-image. What may be called the animal tales synthesize the two previous modes with symbolism, fable, and myth. I call this more recent mode animal tales because Ferguson, as we have already seen, incorporates tortoises, bulls, mermaids (who are, after all, half fish), and, above all, rabbits. Whether he intends it or not, these animal figures, while providing formal and organic elements, also suggest folkloric and fabulous narratives that are both playful and Jungian.

Ferguson began in clay under the Leach/Hamada era, and although he tuned into the Voulkos assimilation or reflection of Abstract Expressionism, he consciously ignored the subsequent art world influences on clay—Funk and Pop. Thus he escaped the tomfoolery of one and the slickness of the other, preferring, it would appear, to take a second look at ritual and commemorative clay: unusable teapots, urns, and trophies all in some way related to town-hall memorials and cemetery statuary. This latter period, I feel, points to the future of ceramics: no more art-world catch-up. No more attempts to disguise the material and its traditions, now that ceramicists are secure in the belief that ceramics can also be art without always imitating what their sculpture and painting neighbors across the hall are up to. Ferguson has shown the way. The way of art is the way of the hare and the bull: full, bounding leaps into the void, along with stand-your-ground stubbornness.

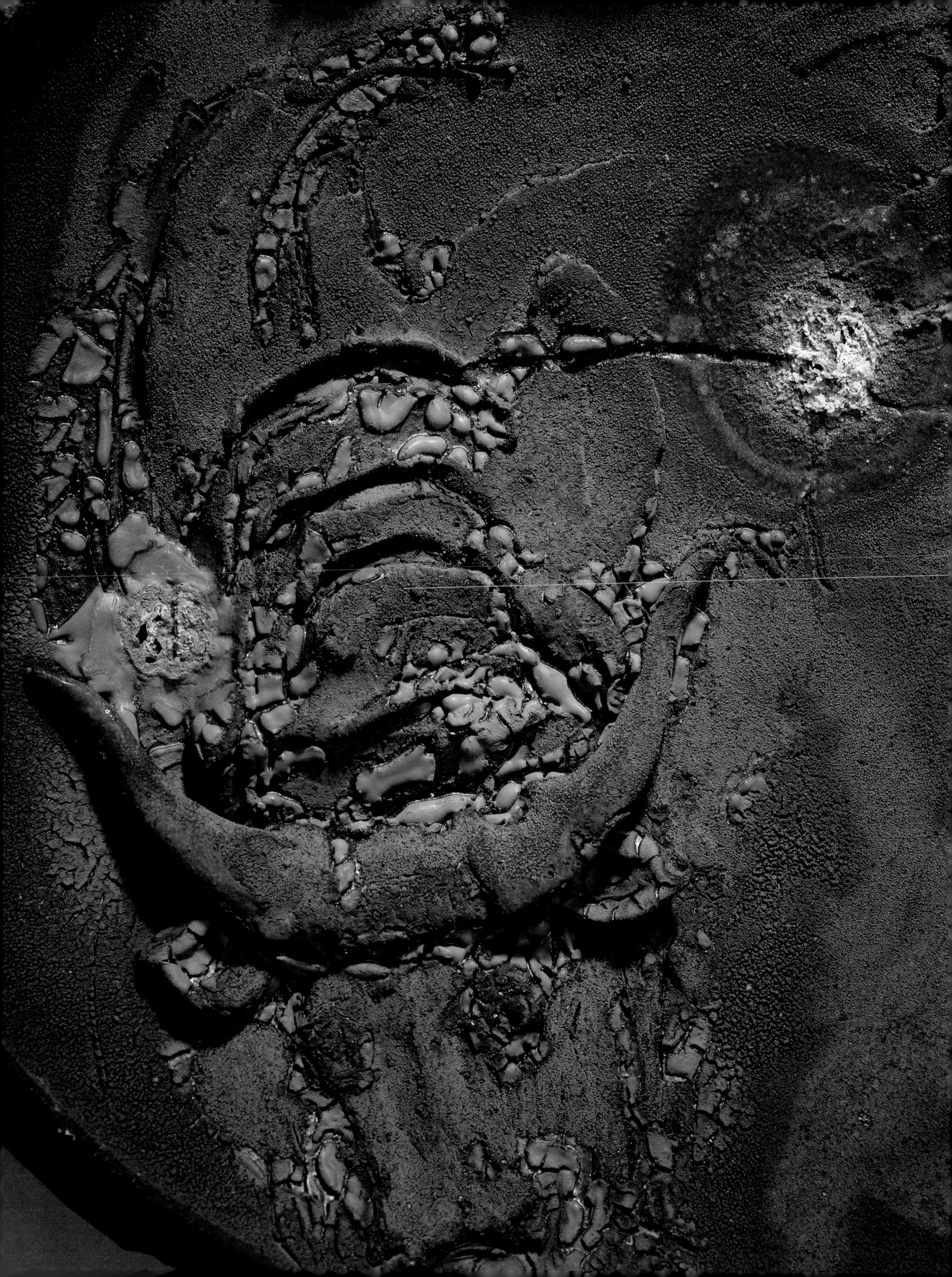

DIGGING A DEEP WELL

KEN FERGUSON

How do you summarize a lifetime of experiences, ideas and contributions? What follows is a combination of writings and conversations that attempt to highlight Ken Ferguson's most formative experiences that enriched his life, heightened his sensitivity, and deepened his understanding.

Hands

Nowadays, when I walk into the classroom, I'm always a bit apprehensive. I've been told that students today only want to work with computers.

When I started art school, all we had to work with were our hands. In 1948 people wondered, "Did anybody in my family use their hands? Was there anybody that was a seamstress, was there anybody who was a stonemason, or an artist of any kind?" We would look back and see that most people had someone in their family who did some hand work.

Our hands served us well. We had to have a steady hand to use a litho crayon, charcoal, and a hard lead pencil. We drew on a hard Wattman board, with very hard pencils, trying to build the drawing to almost black. One of our projects was to draw Roman capitals in ink on paper, no mistakes. This is difficult, a little slip, and you've got a mess, then you start over. Most of the class made them too heavy, with sumptuous, sexy, curvy lines. They really were a much more beautiful thing when they were thin. The challenge really wasn't to avoid making a slip. The challenge was "Do you have and understand a beautiful idea."

I am very curious about hands and how hands help develop the brain. It intrigues me that we, as potters, use our hands to manipulate clay seemingly a little more than other types of artists and craftspeople. It probably is not really true but potters feel that way. When working with clay, you're using your hands with force, and at the same time, your touch is delicate and sensitive. You have to have a feeling for it. When you learn how to throw a pot, you don't have to see if it's on center, you can feel it with your hands. You feel this clay moving through your hands and your fingers. It is very important that you have a good feeling for it and don't try to intellectualize it—just let it happen. Bob Turner said that when he throws, he likes to have it so quiet that he can hear it; he can hear the clay going through his hands; he can hear the moving of the clay. Voulkos was wonderful to watch—never lost a piece of clay. Once he started, it went where he wanted. In other words, you can't put too much pressure, but you have to put some pressure, and you have to have a feel for it. Now I can practically sit down at the wheel, grab a piece of clay, not even look at it and make a pot. I know where it's going, and what it's doing. I can tell if it's going to be too dry, too wet, too soft, if is there a lump, or if there is a problem coming up. I can just tell. I reached a point where I really got in touch with my hands.

Digging a Deep Well

My students have often heard me say "You have to dig a deep well."

The problem people have understanding the phrase "digging a deep well" is that people don't realize that it doesn't have to be within the world of ceramics, and it doesn't have to be about art. "Digging a deep well" is an experience, a challenge, something you've done or that you've faced which forced you to make a decision. You had to decide where to focus. Are you going to get the best of it, or is it going to get the best of you? These things make you a stronger, more sensitive, more passionate person; a person, willing to be tolerant and understanding, able to focus on work and less critical of other's work.

It has to do with intellectual curiosity. An afternoon spent by observing a phenomena of nature and then drawing it, studying it, examining it, trying to figure out how it happens, why it happens and the answers to all of those questions. You go outside of yourself. You have a new experience, and you try to understand it.

The best thing an art school can do is to push its students to do what they don't want to do. Rick Hensley, a former student of mine, went to graduate school at the Rhode Island School of Design. There he was pushed to make a lot of sculpture and things that he wasn't crazy about. He told me, "I kept thinking, 'I want to make pots and these people don't want to help me with my pots.' " Afterwards Hensley discovered that he made better pots because he had made all these other things. He had solved other problems beside the attachment of a handle and the fit of a lid. He said, "It made the process of making pottery more fun and my pottery better."

I remember one day when John Wood was at our house. He spent three hours on the patio with a couple of leaves from an oak tree, studying them, drawing them, looking at acorns, turning them over, feeling them, looking at the many leaves on the tree. He was just curious. He thought, "Why are these leaves shaped this way? What is the whole purpose here?" A leaf that stays on the tree all winter intrigued him. "Why would the leaf stay on all winter and pop off when it was time for a new leaf?" he asked. People who think that way are searching. They're the people who make great discoveries. But you don't have to make great discoveries to improve yourself. They can be things just for you. Private things.

Why is it important to dig that deep well? Long term, the reason is that you may run out of ideas. It's very easy to do. There will be a demand on you for new ideas. It's one of the most hateful, terrible things about the art world—artists are always asked, "Any new things?"

You want new ideas to come out, and you hope they do. I remember talking to Akio Takamori, and he said, "I don't have any ideas. I'm out. I ran out. I just reached a point where I don't have any new ideas. What do I do?" I told him to go back and revisit his old ideas. Look at them and think, "Did I really take this as far as I could? Is there more to it?" You want to have these ideas—they keep you going.

What are some of the steps in digging my well?

PLATE 48

PLATE 49

Japan

In 1952 I was drafted into the Army for service in Korea. Japan was an indoctrination stop before shipping to the combat zone.

When I got to Japan, I was amazed by the country immediately. The trees, the buildings, it was snowing every night, maybe an inch and a half and was almost gone by noon. It was beautiful.

I had an MOS (military occupational specialty) as a clerk typist. While preparing for transfer to Korea, a friend from high school pulled me out of the line and arranged for me to work at headquarters in Japan. My first day my commanding officer said, "We're filled up with clerk typists, I see you went to art school, could you be a draftsman?" I agreed. "Well," he said, "we need a draftsman in the signal corp." Right away that's what I became. I was in a room that was top-secret. One wall was covered with big relief maps with the location of all the U.S. communication systems in Korea and Japan. I was in this room which you had to ring a bell to get in, and I got top-secret clearance, believe it or not. Cryptographers worked next door. To get to these cryptographers, you had to pass by me. I didn't have much work to do. My Major said, "Put a very complex drawing on your drawing board, half-finished, and get the tools out and everything every day, so you can get going on it if you have to but leave it alone because I don't know what to have you do, and I'm too busy to think up something." That's the army.

While stationed in Japan, I started seeing things. I wanted to understand the culture: their great sense of graphics and design, the way they lived. Their writing was clean, very neat. Everything was organized. They have a strong love of nature. I saw a garden that was nothing but moss—a beautiful thing to see. The kareansui, rock garden, on the grounds of the Ryoan-ji Temple is also beautiful. It was originally designed in A.D. 1450. Three walls of stone and plaster partially surrounded a level area of sand and groups of stones. The sand was carefully raked around the stones. If you don't get the message sitting there for a while, then you're not going to get it. It is so simple; it's just amazing.

Another place of simple beauty is Ise, a Shinto shrine near the Pacific Ocean in a large park not far from Nagoya. There are tall, redwood-like trees, carefully placed stones and many buildings of third-century A.D. architectural style. It is a secluded, sacred place—some buildings are off limits. The main shrine is rebuilt every twenty years. The old buildings are dismantled; new buildings are erected to the same plan and sacred objects are transferred. The entire compound is restored to every detail from the straw roofs to the gilded trim. Each of my visits to Japan coincided with a year of the rebuilding of Ise. I saw it happen three times. As it was rebuilt in '53. I watched them take out one beam at a time, duplicate it, and put it back. Really amazing. Oh, I thought the buildings were just incredible.

I just fell in love with the country. I had gone to Japan thinking I was going to be a stained glass window designer. I hate to tell this to anybody, but I hardly thought of it. There are no stained glass windows in Japan. In fact I don't think I ever thought, "I can't wait to get back and design stained glass windows." No, it was not going to be a love in my life, not at all.

So being in Japan was very important to me. It was almost too good to be true. I met some great people, I learned how to get along, I learned how to do things I didn't want to do. Don't question it, just do it—which is hard for an artist.

(top left)
Building at Ise Shrine (Shinto), Ise City, Japan 1993

(top right)
Plotting imaginary aggressor. PFC Kenneth R. Ferguson kneeling. Sendai, Japan 1954

(bottom)
Sand garden at Ryoanji zen buddist temple, Kyoto, Japan 1953

The Archie Bray Foundation

Before Gertrude and I were married, we didn't have a firm plan. We agreed we would work together; we would talk about it and see what would happen. I asked, "Should we go to Toledo and take this job at the museum or should we go to the Archie Bray Foundation?" Didn't take long to decide, I took the job at the Archie Bray Foundation in Montana. We thought, "now that's a great adventure." We're going to go out West, we've never been out there. Gertrude's going to see what inspired Zane Grey to write *Riders of the Purple Sage*, and Owen Wister to write *The Virginian.*

At the Bray, my pots were utilitarian, not very expensive, mostly decorated with glazes. In fact the glazing technique was the decoration. Glaze was poured— I couldn't afford the luxury of mixing large vats of glaze for dipping. Economy and speed were important. I made large jars, platters, sets of dishes, pitchers, teapots and various types of baking dishes. I was pleased to be a potter. I did not want to be an artist. My potter friends talked and thought of clays, glazes, kilns, selling, galleries and exhibits. I did everything: mixed clay, stacked and fired kilns, taught classes, and gave a few workshops. My life was filled up.

Archie, Jr. closed the brickyard in 1960 and left for California. We had no warning. Suddenly on a cold Saturday morning, Fritz Gannon, the brickyard's banker, came out in his old clothes. As he stormed into the pottery Fritz asked, "Where is he? Where's Archie?" "I don't know," I said. The people in the office didn't even know. Gannon was about to come unglued. Everything was shut down. After a few days, Jane Hibbard talked with Fritz. Jane was one of the students in the Bray's adult education classes and a member of the bank's board. Jane told him, "These are nice people. It's a good thing. It doesn't hurt or cost anybody anything, and they take care of themselves. They're not living in the lap of luxury." We were living in an old chicken coop that had been fixed up. Anybody willing to stay there, under those conditions, must love the place. Shortly thereafter, Sue Bovey and Joyce MacKay came out and asked, "What do you need?" With the help of some supportive friends, we were able to make it.

We stayed there, of course we stayed. Gertrude and I kept the doors open for others to follow. It was the finest act of our life together.

Las Trampas

Many years later after my visits to Ryoan-ji and Ise, something in our country moved me in a similar way—the adobe church at Las Trampas, New Mexico. The church, built in 1751, continues to serve the people of the mountain community who live near the high road from Santa Fe to Taos.

Las Trampas represents something humble, beautiful, and passionate. People worked right from their heart, used their loving, caressing hands to make that building and covered the building with adobe. They smoothed it down while they put on the adobe.

The furnishings inside are portable. The people put a lot of time into the Christos and Santos. If it rained too much or something happened to the building, they just took the altar, put it someplace else and built another building around it. It was a very simple solution. The people made everything work.

Soetsu Yanagi talked about the Chartres Cathedral in France. He kept saying "that's 'Our Church,' the craftsman's church." I don't agree. Las Trampas is our church. Las Trampas really represents somebody's hands. You look around those buildings, and you'll see handprints. It's the best that the community could do with what it had at that time. It represents complete integrity. Las Trampas represents that purity of crafts of which we see so seldom and of which we were supposed to be a part. That's our beginning.

The Future of Ceramics

> My question to ceramics users, appreciators, collectors, makers, artists, educators, and students is: Do you wish to be one of those people who are asked to leave something behind?

I still believe in learning to throw pots—you get to know the materials—you can express ideas very fast—thrown pieces can be used to hand-build larger pots. If you go through the discipline of learning to throw well, glaze and fire a kiln, you are deeply into the medium. Then you have a product, something people can use and hold in their hands—you can sell it. You can go anywhere from there: continue on the wheel, hand-build, bas relief, casting with plaster molds. It is a broad, wide-open world. You have a foundation on which to build. You don't know where you'll be in twenty years. The wheel is a good way to start.

There were some people who rejected the wheel and worked directly in clay—large sculptures, wall panels. The medium is certainly inclusive. We teach clay to thousands each year. Some very fine work emerges. I am continually fascinated, sometimes in awe, at the clay art being made.

PLATE 50

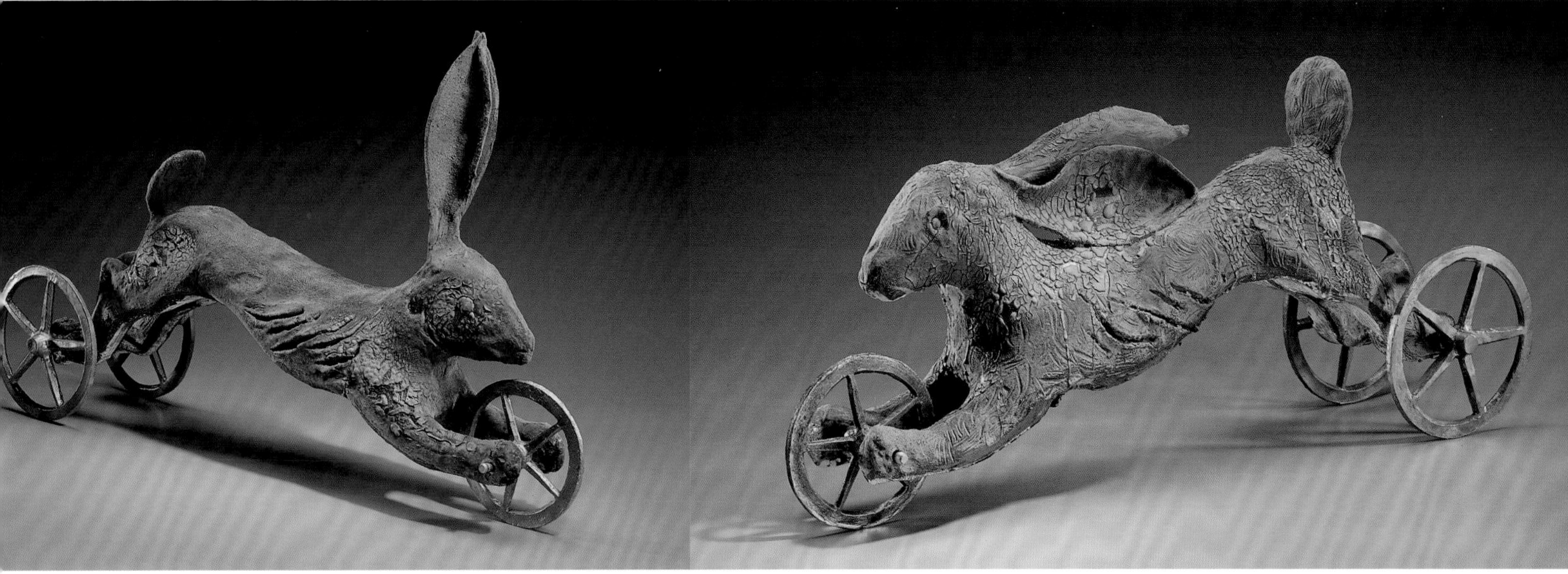

(LEFT TO RIGHT)
PLATE 51, PLATE 52

In the early 40's clay was resurrected, and many people were fascinated with throwing pots. Enough people showed us how to throw and give us a good foundation in this ancient art. I came in the picture in 1955. In no time many people were making pots to use. We reinvented the wheel, built a myriad of kilns, and invented beautiful glazes. Before we knew it, there was a new support industry. Raku, salt and wood kilns; elegant potter's wheels; slab rollers; pug mills, and even ceramic raw materials were available.

Since we started making pots in the 50's, we were trying all kinds of ceramics: throwing on the wheel, casting, jiggering, figures, wall panels, Pop Art, Op Art, found objects.Will all of this repeat itself—or recycle? Will somebody in a future art class, bored with computers, discover the wheel again? When I retired, the wheel thrown pot was passé in many ceramic departments. Wheels were "thrown out the window." Maybe all of this will continue—there is considerable momentum. Right now there are a lot of "thing" makers. And these artists don't represent big ideas—or an idea bigger than themselves.

When I was teaching, students who were hand-builders made life-size figures, other students threw tea bowls, some students worked in plaster while a few combined clay with other materials. Some students were disciplined; some followed the beat of another drum. If they worked hard and had integrity in their work, I encouraged them to remake their world the way they saw it. I wished the best for them. We sought ideas and quality.

Some of my students tried to avoid paying their dues. But oftentimes it still took them ten years to get the visibility they were after. It would have been easier and maybe quicker to pay their dues—like so many others—make pots, sell them, exhibit, try for awards and let the pots evolve as they also grow as artists. It is a natural and a healthy way to get there. There are few shortcuts to success.

Some of the pioneers in clay are passing on. Some were heroes. Their work will be missed. Will there be people to take their place? Of course! As long as freedom to express and experiment exists, new people will make innovative work. The next ceramic artists will come from systems that promote new ideas. Some will be too bold and experimental, and some will be too conservative. I believe there will be people that will want to use their hands doing something different than using a computer keypad. These people will need support. They must not be afraid of failure. Those who believe in themselves are most likely to be tomorrow's leaders. A rigid educational system could not have produced Peter Voulkos.

PLATE 53

PLATE 54

The heightened stature of ceramics in the world of art today has certainly been influenced by these courageous artists who opened doors. But remember, ceramics is not new. Look back to the Mimbres culture of the southwestern U.S., the horse from the Tang Dynasty of China, Jomon vessels of Japan. There has been a continuation of ceramic success: Sevres porcelain, Gaudi architecture in Spain, Medieval English pottery, Japanese folk pottery. It is a long list. Why has the "Art World" taken so long to accept clay? The schools and museums are responsible, in my mind. Ceramics has always been there. The education process has failed us. The fine arts curriculum has little room for ceramics. They say it is a craft, not an art. There must be room for both.

An eloquent argument in the case for ceramics as art came with "Erasing the Line," an essay in the July 28, 1980 *New Yorker*, by Calvin Tompkins, in which he quoted Peter Voulkos:

> If the energy is there, I don't give a damn what you call it. A really fine Japanese teabowl can give you the same kind of excitement you get from painting and sculpture. These distinctions are made because people are not educated. Too bad for them.[1]

Within the past ten years, we have reached a point that may be considered progress for ceramics. Just look at the practice of many galleries engaging in lucrative re-sale of ceramics today. Some of these transactions are of considerable magnitude—pots that

originally sold for $20,000 are reselling for $100,000. Is this a plus for the ceramics world? We can't be sure. On one hand, galleries may concentrate on selling high-price items and spend less time selling lower-priced ceramics. On the other hand, gallery resale has helped change some minds on the matter of ceramics versus fine art.

I believe that all signs point to a future for ceramics. If the young ceramic students can work hard, be patient and continue to believe in themselves; their dreams will come true. They should expect to pay their dues and remember: "The end is nothing, the road is all."[2]

My work has evolved, and at the ripe old age of 76, I still have ideas that I want to see completed. My well yields more than I can use—I have to put some ideas back. I try to be inventive. I have become too careful, afraid to waste time, although the desire to experiment is there. I still love to throw pots. I really enjoy the moving clay under my hands. When I sit at the wheel my back doesn't ache and my hands become steady, I get lost in the clay. It is a great feeling. I taught ceramics for forty years. I looked forward to going to work every day. Helping people by sharing what I knew about ceramics was a pleasure for me. It has given me a great deal of satisfaction when I realize that so many fine students have let me be a part of their lives. I thank all of them with all of my heart.

REMEMBERING KEN

TED ROWLAND

Upon completing work on this book in September 2004, Ken entered the hospital for treatment of cancer. Ken returned home in late December of that year and passed away on December 30, 2004.
The following eulogy was delivered at Ken's Memorial Service on April 2, 2005.

I first met Ken at the Archie Bray Foundation. We had spoken over the phone on several occasions. I knew his work and was familiar with the stories about him, but we had never met.

He was sitting on a stump, wearing one of those straw hats, sweating in the sun. I approached, offered my hand and introduced myself. His grip was softer than I expected, and he didn't look directly at me. After exhausting all attempts at polite conversation, the grip tightened, he drew me closer, looked me in the eyes and said, "You've never thrown a pot. You need to throw a pot if you're going to do this." And I became a believer.

Everyone who counted Ken as a friend shares a similar, defining experience—a moment when we entered his confidence and gained his counsel.

In an age of political correctness, when opinions are measured and words are couched, Ken bellowed. Ken could move from the profane to heart-felt compassion, from the ribald to the spiritual, without slowing down.

Ken didn't suffer fools. He gave his time, energy and direction where he saw potential. It wasn't always comfortable; it was meant to transform. The defining events in his life, his service in Japan, college at Carnegie Tech and Alfred, his time at the Archie Bray Foundation, and the move to Kansas City, all took Ken from his comfort zone. He wanted to shock us from our comfort zones, to explore new ground. That's what made him a great teacher.

An early morning phone call on Sunday usually meant something was bothering Ken. He wanted to make sure we understood the importance of the issue, shared his sense of urgency and grasped the details. In an odd way, that booming voice was reassuring—it meant we were part of his family.

Ken liked to punctuate the conversation with quotations or questions. One of his favorites was "Will you be asked to leave something behind?" This wasn't just a rhetorical question. To Ken, this was a challenge to guide every day; this was the standard to which everyone should be held.

There is a temptation, with any artist's passing, to list the collections that hold his or her work as physical proof that something has been left behind. With Ken, that answer fails to recognize his intellect, his complexity, his curiosity, his contradictions, his energy, his insecurities, and his passions. Ken changed what we saw; he changed how we saw it; he changed us.

I will always think of Ken as a glacier—a seemingly immovable, yet unstoppable force of nature, whose surface masks the creative process. And it's only with his passing that we can appreciate the landscape he left behind.

ACKNOWLEDGEMENTS

Working with Ken on this book was a rare opportunity and privilege. His talent, energy and insights are the book's foundation.

It is impossible to talk about Ken without mentioning Gertrude. Her guidance kept this project true to Ken's vision.

Any publishing project is a collaboration, this book is no exception. The publisher would like to thank the following individuals for their advice and support, without which, this project could not have been produced.

Ken & Gertrude Ferguson
Russell Ferguson
Charles Ferguson
Emily Ferguson Regis
Coy & Margaret Rowland
Garth Clark & Mark Del Vecchio
John O'Brien
Emily Eddins
Joann Rapp
Leslie Ferrin
Harry Dennis
Irv Tepper
Cristina Hernández Villalón
Russ Yaquinto

WRITER'S BIOGRAPHIES

GARTH CLARK is a noted historian and critic. In addition, he, with his partner Mark Del Vecchio, represented Ken Ferguson's work for two decades through their galleries in Los Angeles, Kansas City and New York. He has edited, authored, and co-authored over forty books on ceramic art. Amongst his many awards and honors is the prestigious 2005 Mather Award for Distinguished Achievement in Critical Writing from the College Art Association.

JOHN PERREAULT is a past president of the United States section of the International Association of Art Critics (AICA-USA) and was the curator at the Everson Museum of Art and the American Craft Museum (now the Museum of Arts & Design). Currently, he is a director of The Louis Comfort Tiffany Foundation and writes art criticism weekly for ArtsJournal.com in a section entitled Artopia.

TED ROWLAND is a ceramic collector and friend of the Ferguson family.

PETER von ZIEGESAR is a writer and filmmaker living in New York City. He has written about film and art for many national publications including *DoubleTake, The New York Times, The New York Times Sunday Magazine, Outside, Out, Art in America*, and more recently an essay for the Charlotte Street Fund's tenth anniversary publication. He has also written several screenplays and his short fiction won a PEN Syndicated Fiction Prize. In 1995, along with his wife, Hali Lee, he founded Golden Pig Productions to make documentary films of social and economic importance.

PHOTOGRAPHER'S BIOGRAPHIES

Fine art and portrait photographer, GLORIA BAKER FEINSTEIN received her MA in Photography from the University of Wisconsin in 1979. Her work has since appeared in exhibitions across the country and is included in several prominent collections, including The Nelson-Atkins Museum of Art, the Center for Creative Photography, the High Museum of Art, the University of Kentucky Art Museum and the Harry Ransom Humanities Research Center. She has published two books: *Convergence* and *Among the Ashes*, both of which feature her images and her writing. Feinstein is represented by the Dolphin Gallery in Kansas City.

E.G. SCHEMPF has built a career photographing fine art for galleries, museums, artists, and private collectors over the past twenty-five years. Based in Kansas City, his clients have included The Nelson-Atkins Museum of Art, the Hallmark Fine Arts Collection, Mid-America Arts Alliance, the Dolphin Gallery and Grand Arts galleries, and locally, nationally and internationally recognized artists. His work has appeared in *Art in America, Ceramics Monthly, ArtNews, FiberArts* and *Beadwork* magazines. He is a graduate of Kansas City Art Institute and holds a B.F.A. in Photography.

NOTES

PETER von ZIEGESAR

The author wishes to use this opportunity to thank Ken Ferguson's many former students who generously allowed me to interview them by telephone and in person during the months of February, March, and April 2004. They are (roughly in the order I interviewed them): Cary Esser, Allan Winkler, Stan Welsh, Irvin Tepper, Richard Notkin, Kurt Weiser, Akio Takamori, Sarah Jaeger, Silvie Granatelli, Josh Deweese, Richard Hensley, Donna Polseno, John Gill, and James Watkins. In addition, I'd like to thank Victor Babu, Ferguson's former colleague in the Ceramics Department of the Kansas City Art Institute. Without all of their clear insights and sharp recollections of Ken Ferguson's teaching years—fueled by their obviously still strong affection for and awe of their former instructor—this article would have been impossible to write. All quotations of Ferguson's former students stem from these conversations and are attributed in the text.

In addition, the author interviewed Ferguson at his home and studio in Shawnee, Kansas, on February 3 and 4, 2004. Several subsequent telephone calls helped me to clarify specific points or add new insights. Unless otherwise specified, all quotations from Ferguson come from these conversations.

1. Attributed to Peter Voulkos by Ken Ferguson.
2. Peter von Ziegesar, "The Pot is the Man: Kenneth Ferguson," *American Ceramics*, 10 (winter, 1993): 20.
3. Ann Shaner and Gertrude Ferguson, "Conjugal Relationships: Ann Shaner and Gertrude Ferguson, Wives," *The Studio Potter* 20. No. 1 (December 1991): 58-62.
4. Interview with Russell Ferguson by the author, February 5, 2004. Russell's insights and recollections concerning Helena and the early years in Kansas City were invaluable.
5. T. S. Eliot, "The Love Song of J. Alfred Prufrock," (1919) in *Reading About the World, Volume 2*, ed. by Paul Brians, Mary Gallwey, Douglas Hughes, Azfar Hussain, Richard Law, Michael Myers, Michael Neville, Roger Schlesinger, Alice Spitzer, and Susan Swan (New York: Harcourt Brace Custom Books, 1999).
6. Kenneth Ferguson, "A High Altitude Wood-Burning Kiln," *The Studio Potter* 1, No. 11 (December 1982): 36.
7. David Lewis, *Warren MacKenzie: An American Potter* (New York: Kodansha International, 1991): 31.
8. In 1991, MacKenzie wrote, "When function and need are ignored in favor of technique and the 'cult of the personality,' I feel that it presages a decline of culture."
9. Wallace Stevens, "Of Mere Being" from Eleanor Cook, *Poetry, Word-Play, and Word-War in Wallace Steven* (Princeton University Press, 1998). Retrieved February 20, 2007 from Modern American Poetry: http://www.english.uiuc.edu/maps/poets/s_z/stevens/mere.htm

JOHN PERREAULT

1. Edward Lebow, *The Pottery of Ken Ferguson* (Kansas City: The Nelson-Atkins Museum of Art, 1995). This essay and von Ziegesar's are essential to understanding Ferguson's work. Hopefully, the present writer can add something to this excellent work.
2. Peter von Ziegesar, "The Pot is the Man: Kenneth Ferguson." *American Ceramics* 10 (winter 1993).
3. Kenneth Ferguson, "A High Altitude Wood-Burning Kiln," *The Studio Potter* 1, No. 11 (December 1982): 36.
4. von Ziegesar, op.cit.
5. Lebow, op.cit.
6. In conversation with Ferguson

KEN FERGUSON

1. Calvin Tompkins, "Erasing the Line," *The New Yorker* 56, No. 23 (July 28, 1980): 84, 87.
2. Jules Michelet, in Willa Cather "Joseph and His Brothers," *Not Under Forty* (New York: Knopf, 1936): 96-122.

CATALOGUE

PLATE 01
Pitcher. 1960
Stoneware, Val Cushing tan glaze, 13.625" x 4.75" x 6.25"
Collection Joan Lincoln
Photographer Al Abrams, Phoenix

PLATE 02
Butter Dish. 1961
Stoneware, Meloy black glaze, 3.625" x 8.125"
Collection Ken & Gertrude Ferguson
Photographer E.G. Schempf

PLATE 03
Covered Jar. 1964
Stoneware, Hyrum Dam glaze, 6.125" x 4.375"
Collection Russell Ferguson
Photographer E.G. Schempf

PLATE 04
Cookie Jar. 1975
Stoneware, Val Cushing tan glaze, 13.5" x 12"
Collection Ken & Gertrude Ferguson
Photographer E.G. Schempf

PLATE 05
Batter Bowl. 1977
Stoneware, Val Cushing tan glaze, 5.5" x 13.5"
Collection Ken & Gertrude Ferguson
Photographer E.G. Schempf

PLATE 06
Vase. 1999
Wood fired porcelain, 12.25" x 6.5"
Dolphin Gallery
Photographer E.G. Schempf

PLATE 07
Vase. 1999
Wood fired porcelain, 10.25" x 6.5"
Dolphin Gallery
Photographer E.G. Schempf

PLATE 08
Vase. 1999
Wood fired porcelain, 12" x 5.75"
Dolphin Gallery
Photographer E.G. Schempf

PLATE 09
Slump Jar. 1977
Wood fired stoneware, Shino glaze, 11.25" x 8"
Collection Ken & Gertrude Ferguson
Photographer E.G. Schempf

PLATE 10
Casserole. 1980
Porcelain, red glaze, 8.75" x 11.5"
Collection Ken & Gertrude Ferguson
Photographer E.G. Schempf

PLATE 11
Oribe Water Pot.
11.5" x 9.5" x 7.25"
Collection Ken & Gertrude Ferguson
Photographer E.G. Schempf

PLATE 12
Korean Tea Bowl.
2.5" x 5.5"
Collection Ken & Gertrude Ferguson
Photographer E.G. Schempf

PLATE 13
Mermaid Platter. 1986
Salt fired porcelain, blue spots, 20" x 18" x 3.5"
Collection Don Jahn
Photographer E.G. Schempf

PLATE 14
Adam & Eve Platter. 1981
Salt fired porcelain, cobalt drawing, 19" x 2.5"
Private Collection
Photographer Unknown

PLATE 15
Basket with Braided Handle. 1982
Stoneware, Shino glaze, 20" x 9.75"
Private Collection
Photographer Unknown

PLATE 16
Hare Platter. 1982
Salt fired porcelain, 23" x 19" x 4.5"
Collection Ken & Gertrude Ferguson
Photographer E.G. Schempf

PLATE 17
Nude Platter. 1984
Salt fired porcelain, blue spots, 22.75" x 4.25"
Collection Ken & Gertrude Ferguson
Photographer E.G. Schempf

PLATE 18
Nude Platter. 1985
Porcelain, cobalt drawing, 21" x 3.5"
Collection Lennie Berkowitz
Photographer E.G. Schempf

CATALOGUE CONTINUED

PLATE 19
Adam & Eve Platter. 1985
Salt fired porcelain, Osage spot, 22.5" x 4"
Collection Ken & Gertrude Ferguson
Photographer E.G. Schempf

PLATE 20
Hare Basket. 1985
Black stoneware, residual salt, 13" x 15.5"
Collection Adrian & Constance Saxe
Photographer Anthony Cunha

PLATE 21
Teapot. 1987
Salt fired porcelain, 20" x 12" x 10"
Collection Ken & Gertrude Ferguson
Photographer E.G. Schempf

PLATE 22
Hare Handle Teapot. 1987
Black stoneware, residual salt, Osage spot, 22.5" x 9" x 12"
Collection Ken & Gertrude Ferguson
Photographer E.G. Schempf

PLATE 23
Slump Jar. 1978
Stoneware, Mashiko slip, 12.5" x 8"
Collection R.L.Pfannebecker
Photographer Jack Ramsdale

PLATE 24
Nude Platter. 1987
Salt fired porcelain, 21" x 3.5"
Collection Lennie Berkowitz
Photographer E.G. Schempf

PLATE 25
Parade Pot. 1989
Black stoneware, chrome slip, 17" x 14.5"
Private Collection
Photographer E.G. Schempf

PLATE 26
Hare Platter. 1990
Black stoneware, chrome slip, 22.25" x 18.75" x 4.5"
Collection Lennie Berkowitz
Photographer E.G. Schempf

PLATE 27
Parade Pot. 1990
Black stoneware, residual salt, 15.25" x 18" x 18"
Collection Joanne Rapp
Photographer Al Abrams, Phoenix

PLATE 28
Hare Handle Teapot. 1991
Black stoneware, chrome slip, 23.25" x 12"x 7 3/4"
Collection Robert & Lynda Shapiro
Photographer E.G. Schempf

PLATE 29
Shigaraki Slump Jar. 1993
Shigaraki clay, wood fired, 22" x 12"
Collection Ken & Gertrude Ferguson
Photographer E.G. Schempf

PLATE 30
Shigaraki Hare Platter. 1993
Shigaraki clay, wood fired, Osage spot, 20" x 18.5" x 4"
Collection Ken & Gertrude Ferguson
Photographer E.G. Schempf

PLATE 31
Tea Bowl. 2003
Wood fired porcelain, 3" x 5"
Dolphin Gallery
Photographer E.G. Schempf

PLATE 32
Tea Bowl. 1993
Black stoneware, black glaze, 3.75" x 4.5"
Collection Ken & Gertrude Ferguson
Photographer E.G. Schempf

PLATE 33
Mermaid Platter. 1994
Black stoneware, chrome slip, Osage spot, 21" x 18.75" x 4"
Dolphin Gallery
Photographer E.G. Schempf

PLATE 34
Hare Handle Teapot. 1995
Black stoneware, chrome slip, 22.5" x 9" x 11.5"
Collection Roger & Joni Cohen
Photographer E.G. Schempf

PLATE 35
Four-Legged Tureen. 1996
Black stoneware, chrome slip, 19" x 17" x 17"
Collection Kyorak & Ke-Sook Lee
Photographer E.G. Schempf

PLATE 36
Mermaid Udder Jar. 1996
Black stoneware, chrome slip, 24.5" x 12" x 12"
Collection Emily Eddins
Photographer E.G. Schempf

PLATE 37
Hare Handle Basket. 1997
Black stoneware, chrome slip, Osage spot, 27" x 16" x 14"
Collection William Shapiro
Photographer E.G. Schempf

PLATE 38
Slump Jar on Wood Pedestal. 1998
Black stoneware, chrome slip, stained pine pedestal, 30.5" x 13.5"
Dolphin Gallery
Photographer E.G. Schempf

PLATE 39
Mermaid Basket with Dolphins. 1998
Black stoneware, chrome slip, 12"x 16.75" x 12.25"
Collection John O'Brien
Photographer E.G. Schempf

PLATE 40
Slump Jar. 1998
Black stoneware, chrome slip, 32.5" x 12"
Collection Tom Waldeck
Photographer Ken Ferguson

PLATE 41
Adam & Eve Platter. 1998
Black stoneware, chrome slip, Osage spot,
22.25" x 20.5" x 4.5"
Collection Robert & Lynda Shapiro
Photographer E.G. Schempf

PLATE 42
Vase. 1999
Wood fired porcelain, 11" x 5"
Dolphin Gallery
Photographer E.G. Schempf

PLATE 43
3 Vases 1999
Wood fired porcelain
Dolphin Gallery
Photographer E.G. Schempf

PLATE 44
Tripod Teapot. 1999
Black stoneware, chrome slip, 20.5" x 14.5" x 10"
Collection Roger & Joni Cohen
Photographer E.G. Schempf

PLATE 45
Tri-Udder Pouring Vessel with Mermaid. 1999
Black stoneware, chrome slip, 19.5" x 13" x 16"
Collection Leslie Lerner
Photographer E.G. Schempf

PLATE 46
Fox and Hare Jar. 2000
Black stoneware, chrome slip, 27" x 13"
Collection David Hughes
Photographer E.G. Schempf

PLATE 47
Hare Basket. 2001
Black stoneware, chrome slip, Osage spot,
15.5" x 19" x 12.75"
Collection Robert & Lynda Shapiro
Photographer E.G. Schempf

PLATE 48
Red Bull. 2002
Black stoneware, red glaze, gold leaf, bronze
wheels, brass chain, 13.75" x 17" x 9"
Collection Bob Bernstein
Photographer E.G. Schempf

PLATE 49
Udder Jar with Bulls. 2002
Black stoneware, chrome slip, 15" x 10" x 10"
Collection Keith & Laura Tucker
Photographer E.G. Schempf

PLATE 50
Bull Platter. 2003
Black stoneware, chrome slip, Osage spot,
18.5" x 20.25" x 3.5"
Collection Steve & Barbara Abend
Photographer E.G. Schempf

PLATE 51
Hare on Wheels. 2003
Black stoneware, chrome slip, bronze wheels,
17" x 28.5" x 7"
Collection Luke & Janet LeTourneau
Photographer E.G. Schempf

PLATE 52
Hare on Wheels. 2003
Black stoneware, chrome slip, bronze wheels,
13" x 28.5" x 7"
Collection Kathleen Collins
Photographer E.G. Schempf

PLATE 53
Cup with Hare Handle. 2003
Black stoneware, chrome slip, 4.75" x 8"
Dolphin Gallery
Photographer E.G. Schempf

PLATE 54
Black Bull. 2003
Black stoneware, chrome slip, gold leaf, bronze
cart and wheels, brass chain, 13.5" x 11" x 22"
Dolphin Gallery
Photographer E.G. Schempf

PLATE 55
Udder Jar with Bulls. 2003
Black stoneware, chrome slip, gold leaf,
15.75" x 13" x 13"
Collection Ted Rowland
Photographer E.G. Schempf